ADVANCING FAMILY
PRESERVATION PRACTICE

OTHER RECENT VOLUMES IN THE
SAGE FOCUS EDITIONS

ADVANCING FAMILY PRESERVATION PRACTICE

E. Susan Morton
R. Kevin Grigsby
editors

SAGE PUBLICATIONS
International Educational and Professional Publisher
Newbury Park   London   New Delhi

11-1-95

For information address:

SAGE Publications, Inc.
2455 Teller Road
Newbury Park, California 91320

SAGE Publications Ltd.
6 Bonhill Street
London EC2A 4PU
United Kingdom

SAGE Publications India Pvt. Ltd.
M-32 Market
Greater Kailash I
New Delhi 110 048 India

Printed in the United States of America

Library of Congress Cataloging-in-Publication Data

Advancing family preservation practice/ E. Susan Morton, R. Kevin
Grigsby, editors.
        p. cm. —(Sage focus editions: 150)
    Includes bibliographical references and index.
    ISBN 0-8039-4570-1. (cl.) —ISBN 0-8039-4571-X (pbk.)
    1. Family services—United States. 2. Child welfare—United
States. I. Morton, E. Susan. II. Grigsby, R. Kevin.
HV699.A43 1993   92-33020
362.7'1'0973—dc20

93 94 95 96   10 9 8 7 6 5 4 3 2 1

Sage Production Editor: Diane S. Foster

Contents

Introduction

In the past 3 years, the field of Intensive Family Preservation Services (IFPS) has seen a dramatic increase in the publication of books and book chapters related to the subject (Adnopoz, Grigsby, & Nagler, 1991; Cole & Duva, 1990; Tracy, Haapala, Kinney, & Pecora, 1991; Wells & Biegel, 1991; Whittaker, Kinney, Tracy, & Booth, 1990; Yuan & Rivest, 1990). Generally, these recently published works either describe IFPS programs (Adnopoz et al., 1991; Kinney, Haapala, Booth, & Leavitt, 1990) or are discussions of program evaluations or evaluation-related issues (see especially Yuan & Rivest, 1990 and Wells & Biegel, 1991). Tracy et al. (1991) have provided a somewhat different publication in that they offer what is described as "An Instructional Sourcebook" that appears to be designed to help others learn about IFPS. All of these publications have been valuable contributions to the literature as they have begun to lay the groundwork for the initiation and promulgation of IFPS programs and program evaluation. One troubling aspect of the literature to date, however, is that there appears to be little description of how IFPS programs have changed or evolved over time. After all, IFPS programs have been in existence for nearly two decades. Surely there have been changes that have taken place as programs have "lived through" the past 20 years. As IFPS practitioners, supervisors, trainers, and evaluators, we became intrigued with the idea that IFPS services have "advanced" since their inception. This book represents our attempt to answer the question of "What has happened over time to the initiation, development, implementation, and evaluation of Intensive Family Preservation Services in the United States?" Further questions include the following:

Are the same theories in use now that were in use years ago?

Has the relationship between Child Protective Services and IFPS programs changed in states that offer IFPS?

Have different or better models of service evolved?

Are the families that are being served at present the same types of families that have been served in the past or are there "special populations" that are in need of IFPS services?

Have the program objectives changed (over time) as IFPS programs have been in operation?

How have IFPS programs evolved in states that have offered IFPS for several years?

What types of families don't seem to respond to IFPS?

In order to answer these and other questions, we called upon authors from around the United States to offer their responses based upon their own experiences as practitioners, administrators, and evaluators. We feel that their responses speak for themselves as they offer a succinct description of how Intensive Family Preservation Services have evolved over the last two decades, and of how they may continue to be advanced and refined through careful scrutiny and evaluation. It is our hope as the editors of this volume, that we offer an optimistic yet careful discussion of the evolution of IFPS with the hope that practitioners, administrators, and evaluators will incorporate the experience and knowledge of others who have been involved with IFPS programs as they have "advanced" over time. We do not claim to be offering a detailed history of the IFPS movement, but rather a meaningful commentary related to the questions above. We also hope that this offers students and other persons interested in learning about IFPS exposure to diverse points of view as related to the development, implementation, and evaluation of Intensive Family Preservation Services.

—R. Kevin Grigsby
—E. Susan Morton

References

Adnopoz, D. J., Grigsby R. K., & Nagler, S. F. (1991). Multiproblem families and high-risk children and adolescents: Causes and management. In M. Lewis (Ed.), *Child and adolescent psychiatry: A comprehensive textbook.* Baltimore, MD: Williams & Wilkins.

Cole, E., & Duva, J. (1990). *Family preservation: An orientation for administrators and practitioners.* Washington, DC: Child Welfare League of America.

Kinney, J., Haapala, D. A., Booth, C., & Leavitt, S. (1990). The homebuilders model. In J. K. Whittaker, J. Kinney, E. M. Tracy, & C. Booth (Eds.), *Reaching high-risk families: Intensive family preservation in human services.* Hawthorne, NY: Aldine de Gruyter.

Tracy, E. M., Haapala, D. A., Kinney, J., & Pecora, P. J. (Eds.). (1991). *Intensive family preservation services: An instructional sourcebook.* Cleveland, OH: Case Western Reserve University, Mandel School of Applied Social Science.

Wells, K., & Biegel, D. E. (Eds.). (1991). *Family preservation services: Research and evaluation.* Newbury Park, CA: Sage.

Whittaker, J. K., Kinney, J., Tracy, E. M., & Booth, C. (Eds.). (1990). *Reaching high-risk families: Intensive family preservation in human services.* Hawthorne, NY: Aldine de Gruyter.

Yuan, Y.-Y. T., & Rivest, M. (1990). *Preserving families: Evaluation resources for practitioners and policymakers.* Newbury Park, CA: Sage.

PART 1

Background

1

The Evolution of Family Preservation

E. SUSAN MORTON

Family preservation services are not new. They have their origins in the practice of home visiting and in the history of child welfare in America. Family preservation has evolved from humble beginnings to its professional status today.

The Elizabethans

The phrase *home visiting* is frequently used to describe services provided in the home to an individual or a family. Services encompass the physical, psychological, educational, social, and developmental needs of the client. This system of delivery of care can be traced back to before the Elizabethan era in England. At that time health and social services were provided to paupers in their own homes. These services were usually provided by the church and concerned benevolent wealthy families. By the 17th century public opinion regarding services to poor children and families had shifted. Between 1590 and the early 1600s, a comprehensive series of social welfare reforms known as the Elizabethan Poor Laws were enacted. A system of public relief was created. The practice of "outdoor relief" was replaced with the concept of "indoor relief" or institutional care. Children who were destitute or who came from families who could not adequately care for them were taken to live, work, and be educated in large institutional facilities called almshouses or poorhouses. Few services were provided to the parents

3

of these children (Wasik, Bryant, & Lyons, 1990). Poor adults, the aged, and those unable to care for themselves because of insanity or physical handicaps were sent to houses of refuge or workhouses. There they could live together and work to repay the community for their keep (Datta, 1976).

Florence Nightingale

Despite this change in attitude toward the poor, home visiting continued as a service to the sick. Around the mid-1860s, Florence Nightingale became a champion of home care. She argued that sick people needed not only services to be offered in the home but that these services must be provided by trained nurses (Monteiro, 1985). As a result of her lifelong dedication to home nursing care, particularly for the sick poor, by the end of the 19th century home visiting was a common practice in all of Europe (Buhler-Wilkerson, 1985). Over the years it has expanded to the point that, in Europe, it is now viewed as a government responsibility and all the helping professions including physicians and psychologists provide home visiting services (Wasik et al., 1990). Thanks to Ms. Nightingale's efforts, visiting nurses in this country continue to provide a valuable and vital service for sick people of all ages and socioeconomic backgrounds.

Early Days of America

In the early days of this country no public policy regarding child welfare existed. Children had no rights and were considered important only as they fit into the adult community (Grotberg, 1976). They were viewed as the property of their parents and were valued as an economic resource for the family. Work was viewed as a social good (Datta, 1976). In 1619, Virginia's assembly decided that any person, regardless of age, found idle could and should be bound over to compulsory work (Dulles, 1965). Historical records from Plymouth Colony indicate that children by the time they turned 6 years of age were expected to be "little adults" and work both in and out of the home (Demos, 1972). The practice of apprenticing or indenturing poor, illegitimate, or orphaned children was very popular in Colonial America. Several states including Massachusetts, Virginia, and North Carolina required the practice for all poor children (Grotberg, 1976).

As in England, almshouses were also built for destitute children. No distinction was made between poorhouses and workhouses. Children were grouped together with adults who were sick, disabled, mentally ill, retarded, or criminal. The first of these was built in 1657 in New York. By 1790 almost every coastal municipality had such institutional facilities. Most Americans supported the idea of the almshouses and considered them positive and economical approaches to the care of dependent children since they provided work opportunities for children (Datta, 1976). Little thought or attention was given to providing direct relief services to poor children or their parents in their own homes. This type of service was believed to encourage laziness and unemployment.

The Industrial Revolution

As the population of this country grew due to mass immigration, cities began to experience increased urbanization and economic and social unrest resulting from the Civil War and the Industrial Revolution. Problems such as poverty, crime and delinquency, contagious diseases, overcrowding, and poor sanitation became common. Environmental conditions began to be viewed as leading causes of personal illness and suffering. This shift in thinking resulted in a change in attitude toward the provision of services to children and families. Children who were destitute or from the working poor classes of society were seen as needing to be saved from these social conditions. Children were now seen as possessing innate goodness and were powerless in society. Adults needed to protect and preserve the goodness that children possessed. Writers such as Charles Dickens, Harriet Beecher Stowe, and Bronson Alcott expressed these new found attitudes of societal child mistreatment in their books and essays. America had entered the Age of Rescue (Grotberg, 1976). By the end of the 1870s, the practice of sending children to almshouses or making them indentured servants gradually fell into disuse (Simms, 1991).

Voluntary and public institutions designed to care for dependent children and destitute adults increased—such as the Young Women's Christian Association (YWCA) in 1874 and the Young Men's Christian Association (YMCA) in 1885. In the late 1800s, settlement houses were established in impoverished communities in New York, Boston, Philadelphia, and Chicago. One of the most famous settlement houses was Hull House in Chicago, founded by Jane Addams in 1889. Workers taught hygiene and nutrition; created recreational, cultural, and social programs for people; assisted families in locating better housing; supplied food and clothing to the indigent; and provided support and guidance to families (Addams, 1935/1960).

Teachers began to make home visits. These visiting teachers worked in urban areas to help foster a relationship between the child and his or her family and the school system. Their goal was to reduce truancy, increase scholarship, improve the home environment, and promote an appreciation for education and learning (Levine & Levine, 1970).

Visiting nurses expanded their services and added preventive care for mothers, babies, children, and people suffering from tuberculosis. Home visiting was developing as a practice of the service delivery system in the areas of health, education, and social services. It would take until the 20th century for it to become an organized integral service in the public welfare system of this country (Wasik et al., 1990).

While services to poor families were increasing, a new idea for the care of abandoned or orphaned children—in the orphanage—was being explored. This movement had begun with religious and small private charity groups back in the mid-1700s. Public institutions soon followed in the 1800s (Bremner, 1971). After allegations of abuse and documentation of poor conditions began to surface, some concerned citizens started to call for alternatives. The public debate as to whether to improve and reform these facilities or to maintain children in homes has raged on for years. In 1853 the Children's Aid Society was established in New York. Its mission was to save indigent children from the perils of city life. Urban destitute children were sent to rural areas in the midwest and upstate New York to live with families who would teach them good work habits and provide good moral training. This created the establishment of the first free foster homes. In 1883, a similar initiative called the Children's Home Society was begun. This statewide voluntary agency in Illinois provided free foster homes for children. Children were seen as contributing family members. Foster families were expected to teach the children the value of hard work and discipline. In return they would receive free child labor. Thus this new form of foster care served the interests of both poor families and families seeking employees (Zelizer, 1985).

By the 1890s, both of these programs had been replicated in many states. Despite this acceptance of foster care as an alternative, children's institutions continued to be an alternative for minority, handicapped, and incorrigible children and infants. Minority children were often considered by white society as being unfit or genetically deviant. All of these youngsters were seen as liabilities because of their perceived uselessness (Datta, 1976).

Eventually the practice of foster family placement was created. This offered an alternative to placing children in orphan asylums. States such as Massachusetts began to pay families board money to care for foster children. No longer were children responsible for paying for their keep. States would now assume the responsibility of paying to ensure the welfare of their needy children (Datta, 1976).

In 1851 the first state statute for adoption was enacted in Massachusetts. By 1929 every state had passed some type of law regarding the adoption of children (Datta, 1976).

Other initiatives to promote services to children soon followed. The first Society for the Prevention of Cruelty to Children was founded in New York in 1874 and later, in 1877, the Charity Organization Society was created. These organizations sought individual reform by recruiting volunteer friendly visitors to go into poor peoples' homes and provide advice and support. This attempt to provide individual case services along with the settlement worker movement served as the context for the development of the social work profession. Gradually this country had begun to develop an awareness of the need to protect the welfare of children. Along with this came the belief that society had the responsibility and the right to intervene in a family's life when the welfare of the children was at risk (Bremner, 1971).

The First White House Conference on Children

In 1909, President Theodore Roosevelt established the First White House Conference on Children. This was the start of a public commitment to assist children by keeping them in their homes and preserving "home life" (Bremner, 1971). "Home life is the highest and finest product of civilization . . . children should not be deprived of it except for urgent and compelling reasons" (Lubove, 1965). Poverty alone should not be a reason to remove children from their homes. Thus the concept of family preservation was born. Despite this support for maintaining children at home, though, the conference was careful to designate only voluntary charity as the means to care for families. Services to children and their families continued to remain scarce and unprofessional. Sadly, actual implementation of family preservation practice did not occur for years to come. Yet, momentum for children's services was building.

The Children's Bureau

The U.S. Children's Bureau (1912), in the Department of Labor and later in 1968 absorbed into the Office of Children and Youth, and the Child Welfare League of America (CWLA) (1915) were organized as a result of the White House conference. With the establishment of the U.S. Children's Bureau there was a congressional recognition of the federal government's responsibility for children. The Bureau became responsible for investigating and reporting upon matters pertaining to the welfare of children, including infant mortality, birth rates, children's institutions, and all legislation affecting children (Coll, 1973).

The first chief of the Bureau was Julia Lathrop, a social worker and former resident of Hull House. She was the first woman to be selected by a U.S. President to head a federal statutory agency (Grotberg, 1976). One of Chief Lathrop's earliest projects was to initiate the first federal child-care publications. Two famous booklets, which offered practical advice to mothers based on the latest knowledge of child development, were *Prenatal Care* (1913) and *Infant Care* (1914) (Weiss, 1985).

The Children's Bureau and other social service agencies were finally able to bring child labor under the control of the federal government in 1938 with the passage of the Fair Labor Standards Act. The Depression had made the threat of child competition for paying work intolerable for adults. Therefore, the Act's intent was to protect the economic security of adults by removing children from the industrial workplace. It provided a floor for wages and a ceiling on the number of work hours in certain industries. It also supported the emergence of school, and the importance of education, as an alternative to work for children under the age of 16. In 1974, the Fair Labor Standards Act was amended to include children employed in agriculture (Finkelstein, 1985).

Eventually the Bureau was able, under the Sheppard-Towner Act of 1921, to administer grant-in-aid to states for maternal and child health care. This was the forerunner of federal funding for direct services to children and families (Bremner, 1971).

Social Security Act of 1935

The passage of the Social Security Act of 1935 provided further assistance to families to care for children. It created the framework for the federal child welfare policies of today. Under this act, Title IV, Grants to States for Aid to Dependent Children (now called AFDC), provides matching funds for state grants to families with dependent children. Title V, which was later subsumed under Title IVb, provides federal funding to develop statewide child welfare services (McGowan, 1990). Title V targeted children who had been neglected, abused, or abandoned as being eligible for social services, not just for financial aid. This changed social policy by creating services for the poor rather than simply providing income for them (Finkelstein, 1985). The United States now had its first skeletal system of public assistance, social insurance, and child welfare services.

By 1967 AFDC recipients also received services including child care, homemaker services, job placement services, and work incentives for parents. This was a shift from income maintenance to service delivery. AFDC and the child welfare provisions eventually were combined in 1974 into Title XX of the Social Security Act. Title XX has become the single largest federal social service program allocating funds to the states for child services (Finkelstein, 1985).

Foster Care

In 1959, the Child Welfare League of America conducted a national study of the foster care system. For years the field of child welfare had remained a small, closed residual system. Services were uneven, discriminatory, and unprofessional (McGowan, 1990). The results of the study were disturbing. The researchers found that children were removed from their homes unnecessarily and as a result of lack of alternatives. Minority and poor children were overrepresented in the system. Once removed, children were often placed in unstable, undesirable settings and the biological parents were largely ignored. Few attempts at reunification of the child with his biological family occurred and adoption was reserved for white infants. In a sense, we had a nation of children adrift with no system of monitoring or planning for their future (Maas & Engler, 1959). These findings fueled the dissatisfaction with the out-of-home placement system. The CWLA responded by encouraging the development of a system of home-based services as a way of preventing many of these placements (Turitz, 1961). Despite the recognition and national concern about the unnecessary and excessive placement of children, this nation's fiscal policies continued to support out-of-home placement services.

The Great Society Initiatives

Gradually, with the 1960s through the 1970s, even more changes came in public opinion and eventual social policy. Research began to support the growing belief of the negative consequences of separating children from their parents (Bowlby, 1973). Anna Freud (1965) documented that the needs of a child include affection, stimulation, and the need for unbroken continuity in caretaking. Child welfare professionals wrote that what was in the best interests of parents was the need for evidence of adequacy as parents; the need for social, economic, and political security and sovereignty; and the need to receive community support and assistance in times of crisis. A general belief was emerging that by meeting the parents' needs, they in turn would be able to meet the needs of their children (Goldstein, Freud, Solnit, & Goldstein, 1973).

The definition of child abuse and neglect was broadened. Modern X-ray techniques were developed to detect old healed fractures and concussions. Medical practitioners began to reexamine children's injuries and burns. In 1962, Kempe published "The Battered Child Syndrome." The concept of the "battered child syndrome" received professional and public acknowledgment. This significantly increased public sensitivity to the signs and symptoms of child maltreatment. Public, voluntary, and professional groups dedicated to protecting and advocating for the interests of children were established, such as the Association of State Offices of Early Child Development and the Children's Defense Fund of the Washington Research Project in 1973. With this advocacy came the initiation of class action law suits designed to protect the rights of children.

At the same time the public began to criticize child welfare agencies for spending large amounts of resources and began to question the quality of care that children were receiving. A consensus on the need for more community-based services emerged. Growing pressure from constituents led to several federal initiatives.

One such initiative was the passage of P.L. 88-164, the Community Mental Health and Mental Retardation Centers Act, in 1963. This was a social policy shift away from long-term out-of-home institutional care for children and adults. Family and community resources were seen as a way to care for persons with special needs (Dore, 1991).

As part of the Great Society program, Headstart legislation for children was passed in the summer of 1965. This legislation encouraged the growth of community action agencies. It also provided for the establishment of summer programs for children less than 5 years of age (Finkelstein, 1985). Today this program includes services for handicapped children ranging in age from 3 to 5 years, and child-care centers.

By the early 1970s there was agreement that community-based services were effective in reducing recidivism among juvenile offenders. Therefore, the Juvenile Justice and Delinquency Prevention Act of 1974 was passed by Congress. Its intent was to keep youths who are status offenders out of institutions in the juvenile justice system and instead send them through family counseling and more community-based alternative programs. The act provided modest funds to improve state juvenile justice systems and create alternatives to traditional institutional facilities (McGowan, 1990).

In response to media attention about child abuse, P.L. 93-247, The Child Abuse Prevention and Treatment Act of 1974 was adopted. The law defines *abuse* as "the physical or mental injury, sexual abuse, negligent treatment or maltreatment of a child under eighteen." The National Center on Child Abuse and Neglect was created as a result to provide funding for demonstration projects involving improving procedures for reporting and investigating complaints of abuse. While the intent of the law was to focus on prevention and treatment, all the accompanying regulations concern only the reporting and investigation aspects. The resulting effect has been to increase the number of children in the protective service system without providing the resources to deal effectively with this growing population (McGowan, 1990).

In 1975, P.L. 94-142, the Education for All Handicapped Children Act was passed; it stated that children should be treated in the least restrictive environments. Eventually, in 1986 Congress passed P.L. 99-457, which amends the previous Education for All Handicapped Act. Building on P.L. 94-142, this new legislation mandated services to children ages 3 to 5 years with disabilities. It also established a state grant program for handicapped infants from birth to age 2. Both parts of this legislation include community-based proactive preventive services to parents and families of these children (Wasik et al., 1990).

An interesting consequence of the deinstitutionalization movement was the growing awareness of the lack of community programs to meet the needs of caregiving families. The Children's Bureau of the Office of Human Development began to encourage the development and establishment of models of home-based services to strengthen families and provide preventive services (Cole & Duva,, 1990). Several private family service agencies across the country in the late seventies began to offer family preservation services. These pioneering programs—such as Homebuilders of Tacoma, Washington—offered a broad array of psychological, educational, and concrete services. This effort represented a shift from an individual to an ecological perspective focusing on the environment as both a source and a solution to people's problems (Whittaker, Schinke, & Gilchrist, 1986).

Finally, in an attempt to develop a comprehensive approach to child welfare policy and practice, Congress passed P.L. 96-272: The Adoption Assistance and Child Welfare Act of 1980. With this law preventive and reunification services were now federally mandated. This law established that for states to be eligible for federal funds they must provide plans to show that "reasonable efforts" were being made to prevent the need for removal of a child from his or her home. If a child were to be removed, then the state must also demonstrate that reasonable efforts were being made to make the child's home safe for return. States were instructed that family preservation services needed to be in the design of those efforts and plans (McGowan, 1990).

In the 1980s, attention also became focused on the grossly inadequate and inappropriate services for emotionally disturbed children and their families. In 1984 the National Institute of Mental Health (NIMH) began an initiative called the Child and Adolescent Service System Program (CASSP) to increase state-level coordination of mental health services to children and adolescents. CASSP began with $1.5 million to provide 10 state grants. It has grown to the point that in 1989 only three states had not received a CASSP grant (Yelton & Friedman, 1991). This program has redefined the role of parents as partners in their children's treatment; supported the development of parent advocacy, education, and support groups; and encouraged states to adopt various service models that provide family preservation services (Stroul & Friedman, 1986).

Child Welfare Policy in the 1990s

Child welfare policy in the United States has dramatically changed and expanded in the past 200 years. Public concern began with the basic needs of life (food, clothing, shelter, and education) for indigent and orphaned children. Today it has expanded to include the psychological welfare, health, and safety of all children. The responsibility for child welfare has expanded beyond small, private charity organizations and individual donations to state and federal government programming and funding. Services now range in scope from direct individual interventions with children to indirect prevention programs with families and communities. Punitive versus remedial approaches, such as removing children from their homes, are being replaced with new policies that emphasize strengthening families so that they can care for their children at home. Accountability has shifted from the small charity organizations to the adoption of national and statewide standards for quality of care. Professional organizations such as the American Professional Society on the Abuse of Children (APSAC) have been established, which are dedicated to monitoring child welfare services.

Intensive Family Preservation in the 1990s

Consequently, there are now more than 200 IFP programs across the United States in the fields of child welfare, mental health, and juvenile justice. These programs reflect a wide range of practice approaches that have been implemented in various forms and to varying degrees. Some are small privately administered community programs while others are public statewide directives.

Family preservation is now a professional service with a system of values, theories, and interventions. Schools of social work, such as the University of Washington and the University of Iowa, and other human service training programs have begun to develop courses and sequences of study specifically designed to prepare students for careers in programs that incorporate the philosophy and techniques of family preservation.

As we enter the last decade of the 20th century it would appear that family preservation is here to stay. From its earliest inception as an idea, it has evolved into an essential specialized component of delivery of services to children who are at risk of placement and to their families. This evolutionary process, however, is not yet complete. As the needs of families and the sociocultural political environment in the Unites States changes, so too will family preservation. The knowledge and insights that have been and will continue to be gained from family preservation programs will serve as a guide for future reforms of the child welfare system.

References

Addams, J. (1960). *A centennial reader.* New York: Macmillan. (Original work published 1935)

Bowlby, J. (1973). *Separation.* New York: Basic Books.

Bremner, R. H. (1971). *Children and youth in America: A documentary history: Vol. II 1886-1932.* Cambridge, MA: Harvard University Press

Buhler-Wilkerson, K. (1985). Public health nursing: In sickness or in health. *American Journal of Public Health, 75,* 1155-1167.

Cole, E., & Duva, J. (1990). *Family preservation: An orientation for administrators and practitioners.* Washington, DC: Child Welfare League of America.

Coll, B. D. (1973). *Perspectives in public welfare.* Washington, DC: U.S. Department of Health, Education and Welfare.

Datta, L. (1976). Watchman, how is it with the child. In E. Grotberg (Ed.), *200 years of children.* Washington, DC: U.S. Department of Health, Education and Welfare.

Demos, J. (1972). *A little commonwealth.* New York: Oxford University Press.

Dore, M. M. (1991). Context and the structure of practice: Implications for research. In K. Wells & D. E. Biegel (Eds.), *Family preservation services: Research and evaluation.* Newbury Park, CA: Sage.

Dulles, F. R. (1965). *A history of recreation.* New York: Appleton-Century-Crofts.

Finkelstein, B. (1985). Uncle Sam and the children: History of government involvement in child rearing. In N. R. Hiner & J. M. Hawes (Eds.), *Growing up in America: Children in historical perspective.* Champaign: University of Illinois Press.

Freud, A. (1965). Safeguarding the emotional health of the child. In J. Goldstein & J. Katz (Eds.), *The family and the law.* New York: Free Press.

Goldstein, J., Freud, A., Solnit, A. J., & Goldstein, S. (Eds.). (1973). *Before the best interests of the child.* New York: Free Press.

Grotberg, E. (1976). Child development. In E. Grotberg (Ed.), *200 years of children.* Washington, DC: U.S. Department of Health, Education and Welfare.

Kempe, C. H. (1962). The battered child syndrome. *Journal of the American Medical Association, 181,* 17-34.

Levine, M., & Levine, A. (1970). *A social history of the helping services: Clinic, court, school, and community.* New York: Appleton-Century-Crofts.

Lubove, R. (1965). *The professional altruist: The emergence of social work as a career 1880-1930.* Cambridge, MA: Harvard University Press.

Maas, H. S., & Engler, R. E., Jr. (1959). *Children in need of parents.* New York: Columbia University Press.

McGowan, B. (1990). Family based services and public policy: Context and implications. In J. K. Whittaker, J. Kinney, E. Tracy, & C. Booth (Eds.), *Reaching high-risk families: Intensive family preservation in human services.* Hawthorne, NY: Aldine de Gruyter.

Monteiro, L. A. (1985). Florence Nightingale on public health nursing. *American Journal of Public Health, 75,* 181-186.

Simms, M. D. (1991, August). Foster children and the foster care system, part I: History and legal structure. *Current Problems in Pediatrics,* pp. 297-321.

Stroul, B. A., & Friedman, R. M., (1986). *A system of care for severely emotionally disturbed children and youth.* Washington, DC: Georgetown University Child Development Center, CASSP Technical Assistance Center.

Turitz, Z. (1961). Obstacles to services for children in their own homes. *Child Welfare, 40*(6), 1-6.

Wasik, B. H., Bryant, D. M., & Lyons, C. M. (1990). *Home visiting: Procedures for helping families.* Newbury Park, CA: Sage.

Weiss, N. P. (1985). Mother, the invention of necessity: Dr. Benjamin Spock's baby and child care. In N. R. Hiner & J. M. Hawes (Eds.), *Growing up in America: Children in historical perspective.* Champaign: University of Illinois Press.

Whittaker, J. K., Schinke, S. P., & Gilchrist, L. D. (1986, December). The ecological paradigm in child, youth, and family services: Implications for policy and practice. *Social Service Review, 60,* 483-503.

Yelton, S., & Friedman, R. (1991). Family preservation services: Their role within the children's mental health system. In K. Wells & D. E. Biegel (Eds.), *Family preservation services: Research and evaluation.* Newbury Park, CA: Sage.

Zelizer, V. A. (1985). *Pricing the priceless child: The changing social value of children.* New York: Basic Books.

2

Theories That Guide Intensive Family Preservation Services

A Second Look

R. KEVIN GRIGSBY

Intensive family preservation services are provided to families with children at imminent risk of out-of-home placement, usually due to neglect or abuse. The trained clinicians that work with these families are in need of practice-relevant theory to guide the intervention with high-risk families that are often plagued with a multitude of problems. Norman Polansky (1986) argues that theory serves a number of functions in applied fields such as intensive family preservation. Theory can guide the clinician by acting as a "mental map" (p. 4) that allows the clinician to know where to start. Theory also helps to organize the work of the clinician, especially through focusing of the clinician's attention on what seems to be significant. Theory also "articulates the learnings of those who have gone before" (p. 6) through general principles that the novice can apply to the unique situation being faced with while working with clients. Finally, theory can help the clinician to better understand the client's behavior and motivation (perhaps unconscious) behind the behavior. In general, theory provides the undergirding of the clinical intervention. In the area of intensive family preservation services (IFPS), several theories are relevant.

Richard Barth (1990) argues that intensive family preservation services "draw upon four major theories for articulating ideal service delivery systems and treatments: crisis intervention theory, family systems theory, social learning theory, and ecological theory" (p. 89). As Barth (1990) provides an excellent in-depth discussion of these four theories and their application to IFPS, only brief descriptions will be provided below.

Crisis Intervention Theory

The origins of "crisis theory" lie in Erich Lindemann's (1944) study of acute grief reactions. From his study of persons who had experienced the recent death of a close relative, Lindemann concluded that grief was a normal reaction to this type of distress and that people reacted to this distress in similar ways. He argued that acute grief could be managed through preventive intervention. Gerald Caplan (1964), a colleague of Lindemann, continued the development of crisis theory as he identified distinct phases in the course of a crisis. Within these phases, crisis presents an opportunity for growth as well as for increased vulnerability. H. J. Parad and Caplan (1960) broadened the theory by applying it to families, and argued that families may experience crisis in ways similar to individuals. As families experience crisis, they are more receptive to outside intervention than they are during times of relative stability. For this reason, IFPS programs intervene with families in crisis as a child is about to be placed outside of the home. In theory, families have the chance to accept the IFPS intervention and emerge from the crisis in a state of greater strength or better health than prior to the crisis. As Barth (1990, p. 92) points out, "evidence that intervening at the point of crisis is most beneficial" is missing. Even so, the use of crisis intervention theory is a cornerstone of family preservation practice.

Family Systems Theory

Family systems theory does not represent a distinct theoretical construct. Rather, several approaches to family therapy comprise this perspective that views families as being "systems" of interconnected relationships that operate according to an "invisible set of functional demands that organizes the ways in which the family interacts" (Minuchin, 1974, p. 51). The family is a system that interacts with the subsystems of the individual members and the suprasystems of the community at large. In working with families who are experiencing problems, the clinician works toward systemic change that improves family functioning and that will maintain improved family functioning over time. Of utmost importance to IFPS is that this perspective calls for working with the family in the context of the family environment.

Social Learning Theory

Contemporary social learning theory is predicated on the work of Albert Bandura (1977); however, other learning theorists such as Ivan Pavlov, B. F. Skinner, John Dollard and Neal Miller, and George Herbert Mead have contributed to the development of social learning theory. In general, social learning theory asserts that environmental influences, rather than internal or innate states, control learning behavior. Social learning takes place in three stages: exposure to the behaviors of others; acquisition of what has been observed; acceptance of the modeled behavior as a guide for one's own behavior. In short, persons imitate behavior that they observe and they behave as they feel they are expected to behave. Social learning theory and behavioral intervention based upon its principles are recognized within the curricula of most schools of social work (Thyer & Maddox, 1988) and a method of social work practice, behavioral social work, has been derived from social learning theory (Thyer, 1991). IFPS programs such as Homebuilders (Kinney, Haapala, Booth, & Leavitt, 1990) utilize social learning theory to explain dysfunctional behaviors within families and to guide the intervention within those families. As behavioral expectations change and as IFPS therapists teach, model, and reward positive behaviors, overall family functioning improves.

Ecological Theory

As Barth (1990, p. 89) states, "ecological theory is primarily a natural science metaphor for social science-based practice." The ecological orientation in social work is explicated by Germain and Gitterman (1980) and argues that individuals and families can only be understood within the context of their environment. Intervention may require helping clients to develop better skills for dealing with the environment;

however, intervention may also require facilitating changes within the environment of the client. In IFPS programs, this is translated as the provision of both concrete and psychological services. IFPS clinicians advocate for the needs of families and work to empower families within the natural context of their lives. Rather than requiring that families come to an office or clinic, work is home and community based. Meeting the needs of the family within the environment is stressed.

In summary, the professional literature to date regarding IFPS contains little or no dispute with the importance of these theories in guiding the provision of IFPS programs. Experienced family preservation clinicians routinely make use of these theories as they plan and implement services with families that are often fragmented and in the midst of a multitude of problems. As intensive family preservation programs have evolved over the past decade and have been examined critically, these four theories have been viewed as integral to the provision of services, but also as being "incomplete" (Barth, 1990, p. 106). It is unclear whether any single theory or mix of theories will "complete" the framework that will guide intervention that is the most effective for the most families. Other practice-relevant theory may also contribute to the framework that guides intensive family preservation services. In particular, social attachment theory (Ainsworth, 1985, 1989; Bowlby, 1969, 1973, 1980, 1988) and functional theory (Dore, 1990; Smalley, 1971) are congruent with the aforementioned theories that are useful in guiding the provision of intensive family preservation services.

A description of social attachment theory follows and describes how fundamental principles of IFPS have been influenced by the work of social attachment theorists. Functional theory is also discussed and its influence on contemporary family preservation practice is described. Both of these theories have been neglected in the professional literature related to intensive family preservation practice, but appear to be routinely utilized in the provision of intensive family preservation services.

Social Attachment Theory

Continuity of relationships, surroundings, and environmental influence are essential for the child's healthy development (Goldstein, Freud, & Solnit, 1973, p. 31). The relationship that the child forms with its caretakers is of primary importance, because the child develops in the context of this relationship. Disruptions in the continuity of this relationship or failure to establish this relationship may result in various types of problems for the child. Maintaining the continuity of relationships is an important consideration when dealing with children whose caretakers (usually the parents) have failed to meet the needs of the child, as out-of-home placement of children is a possible consequence of this failure. Although out-of-home placement is utilized as a partial solution to this problem, such placement may be traumatic in and of itself and may not always be in the child's best interest. Intensive family preservation programs are cognizant of the potential danger of such placement and therefore seek to prevent them when they are unnecessary. The importance of maintaining the child's relationship with the parent is fundamental to the provision of intensive family preservation services. Social attachment theory offers a framework for understanding the importance of the child-caretaker relationship and the need for continuity. Social attachment theory recognizes the importance of the child-caretaker relationship to the child's healthy development.

John Bowlby (1969, 1973, 1980, 1988) is most often associated with the development of social attachment theory. However, the theory is also grounded in the work of Anna Freud (1965), Mary Ainsworth (1985), René Spitz (1945), Selma Fraiberg (1975), and others. Social attachment theory is focused upon the child-caretaker relationship and postulates that this relationship is necessary and vital to the child's healthy development. The early relationship between the child and the caretaker is seen as having an influence on the child's subsequent relationships with other persons and with the world at large. While attachment to the primary caregivers (who are usually the biological parents) is the foundation of social attachment theory, attachment relationships with other significant persons in the child's life—such as grandparents, siblings—are important considerations in the provision of child welfare services, especially in regard to placement outside of the home. Attachments with siblings, as well as with parents, are important aspects of children's lives and are considered within the scope of social attachment theory. Bank and Kahn (1982) offer an explication of the importance of the child's relationship to siblings in their work on "sibling bonds."

Attachment behavior, in general, is any behavior that results in a person attaining or retaining proximity to another individual. The formation of affectional bonds is biologically rooted and species-characteristic to the human organism, therefore universal in human nature. According to social attachment theory, this behavior is instinctive and has the goal of maintaining proximity to, or communication with, the attachment figure. Attachment behavior leads to the development of affectional (emotional) bonds initially between parent and child, but later in life between adult and adult in sexual-pair relationships, friendship relationships, and relationships between siblings and/or other kin. In fact, "even a child of preschool age may serve as an attachment figure to a younger sibling" (Ainsworth, 1989, p. 714). Caregiving behavior complements the attachment behavior as the caregiver protects the attached organism. This is evident in the parent-child relationship, but is also extended to caregiving in adult-to-adult relationships. The maintenance of an attached relationship, or *bond* as it is sometimes called, is experienced as a source of security. The threat of the loss of the attachment figure elicits anxiety and an actual loss of a bond gives rise to grief and sorrow. In turn, this may give rise to anger. On the other hand, the renewal of a bond is often a source of joy. Attachment behavior continues throughout the life span as children grow into adults and form attachments with other adults. A child's attachment to parents may persist throughout the life span (Ainsworth, 1985). This is fruitful for clinical application, because a threat to the loss of an attachment figure (in this case, a parent) may arouse anxiety and the actual loss of the parent elicits grief. When children are faced with separation from parents in the foster care placement process, the threat of separation is likely to cause anxiety and/or sorrow in the child. Because of this, the decision to remove a child from the family in order to "protect" the child, must be weighed against the possibility of traumatizing the child in the process of out-of-home placement. In addition, the actual loss of siblings, grandparents, and others must also be considered, because the trauma of separation may generate feelings of helplessness, anger, fear of abandonment by the parent, and fear of parental death (Littner, 1967). The child must deal with all of these feelings, as well as with feelings that the foster parents present a potential "threat," which may be experienced by the child unconsciously, but is likely to be expressed as anxiety. Whereas foster care placement is a partial solution to the problem of neglect or abuse, the placement itself is accompanied by its own set of potentially negative consequences. Interruption of the attachment relationship may be detrimental to the child in and of itself. Norman M. Stone and Susan F. Stone (1983) caution protective services workers to "act with the utmost caution in placing children," because interruption of the parent-child relationship through separation of the child "from his or her parents could be only the first in a series of painful separations the child will face" (p. 15).

Applying Social Attachment Theory to IFPS

In relation to the provision of intensive family preservation services, the theory provides great utility. Polansky (1986) describes the marks of a good theory, and social attachment theory appears to meet these standards. Most important, social attachment theory condenses the experience of researchers into general principles that can be applied in various situations. As IFPS services are family-centered, social attachment theory is useful in helping clinicians to maintain a sensitivity to the child's needs in particular, because it is easy to lose sight of the child's needs as services are provided to families that are fragmented and who have a multitude of problems. The fundamental premise of IFPS is that "in most cases, it is best for children to grow up with their natural families" (Kinney et al., 1990, p. 32). This premise is representative of the basic identification of IFPS with the tenets of social attachment theory. The Homebuilders model (Kinney et al., 1990), the Family Support Service model (Adnopoz, Grigsby, & Nagler, 1991), and others (Florida Department of Health, 1990) promote the maintenance of the parent-child and other attachment relationships as these relationships provide the context for the child's growth and development. Unnecessary interruption of these primary attachment relationships may have dire consequences. On the other hand, children who have not formed attachment relationships with primary caregivers or who have received life-threatening injuries at the hands of caretakers are necessarily in need of out-of-home placement and possibly permanent removal from the care of these persons so that these children will have the opportunity to form positive attachment relationships with families who will provide them with the "continuity of relationships, surroundings, and environmental influence" that are essential to the child's healthy development (Goldstein et al., 1973, p. 31). As with the principles of crisis intervention theory, family systems theory, social learning theory, and ecological theory, the principles of social attachment theory are also integral to the provision of intensive family preservation services. Recognition of the importance of this theory and its influence on IFPS has been neglected even though its basic tenets undergird the provision of intensive family preservation services.

Functional Theory

There are several models of intensive family preservation services that have been used in different areas around the United States (Nelson, Landsman, & Deutelbaum (1990). There are a plethora of services that may be offered to children and families that are home-based or family-centered. However, all of the various program models of intensive family preservation programs have common characteristics, common core values, and utilize common techniques. Intensive family preservation services offer "family and home-based time-limited services with the goal of preventing the imminent placement of children in out-of-home care" (Rzepnicki, Scheurman, & Littell, 1991). Common characteristics include:

- immediate response to referrals
- serving children at imminent risk for out-of-home placement
- limiting goals and objectives
- focusing on the family as the unit of intervention
- providing services in the home or community
- offering of both concrete and psychological services
- availability of services outside of traditional (9:00 a.m. to 5:00 p.m.) hours
- offering intensive intervention of 5 to 20 hours per week
- providing services that are short-term in duration (usually 6-12 weeks).

Common core values include the belief that children should remain with their families whenever possible, that families are active agents in the change process, that families are "doing the best that they can" (Kinney et al., 1990), and that intervention should utilize a strength model, rather than deterministic diagnostic models that focus upon family pathology.

Common intervention techniques include home-based counseling; behavioral modeling; the teaching of parenting, communication, and assertiveness skills; and linking clients to other community-based services. Client advocacy is also a mark of intensive family preservation programs.

Functional theory was initially developed at the Pennsylvania School of Social Work in Philadelphia during the 1930s. The first written description of the functional approach appeared in the late 1930s (Taft, 1937) and has evolved over time (Smalley, 1967). Recently, the University of

Pennsylvania School of Social Work (1990) published a review of the development and evolution of the functional approach over the past six decades. Many of the basic principles of functional theory have been incorporated into social work practice in general (Dore, 1990). There are several principles of functional theory:

- Clients are viewed as constantly engaged in the process of growth and change.
- Client empowerment is fundamental.
- A working relationship of mutual respect between the worker and client is developed.
- The client is representative of a population adversely affected by social problems.
- A time-limited, structured process for problem solving is utilized.
- The specific function and purpose of the social agency provide the context for intervention.
- The clinician is cognizant of the dynamics of the change process that occur in the client, the worker, and at times, the agency, in order to advocate for positive change.
- The clinician works to promote planned change within the social service system in order to link clients with needed resources.
- The clinician advocates for a realignment or redistribution of social resources.
- The clinician continuously searches for more effective solutions to complex social problems.

Functional Principles
That Correspond to Principles of IFPS

A number of these principles correspond to the common characteristics, values, and techniques of intensive family preservation services:

1. IFPS programs have a specific function and purpose, which is to prevent unnecessary out-of-home placement.
2. Services are time limited. Dore (1990) suggests that the use of a crisis intervention model reaffirms the emphasis that the functional approach places on the use of time limits as a structuring variable in the process of intervention.

3. The client is emphasized as being an important partner in the change process. As stated by Kinney et al. (1990 p. 36), "clients are our colleagues."

4. Clients are seen as a family unit within a community and as being representative of a population that is being adversely affected by social problems. This perception also draws upon ecological theory, which recognizes the importance of working with clients in the natural environment.

5. The IFPS clinician is responsible for monitoring the process of change that takes places within the clients, the agency, and within themselves in order to advocate for positive change. IFPS workers engage in relationships with clients and assist them in recognizing and building upon their own strengths.

6. IFPS clinicians advocate for their clients within the natural setting (the community) and in doing so are able to promote positive change within the social service system. They advocate for a reallocation and realignment of social services.

7. A strength or growth model is utilized in IFPS that focuses upon dealing with the present-day realities of the family's life, rather than dwelling on past events that may not be relevant to the situation at hand. In IFPS, the centrality of the clients' empowerment is stressed, as in functional theory.

Summary

Several theories appear to be integral to the provision of intensive family preservation services. Crisis intervention theory, family systems theory, social learning theory, and ecological theory have been recognized as fundamental to most IFPS programs. A reexamination of the theoretical undergirding of IFPS does not dispute the importance of these theories. It does appear, however, that the inclusion of two additional theories, social attachment theory and functional theory, is warranted since IFPS programs utilize the principles of these theories in the day-to-day provision of services to families in crisis. Social attachment theory stresses the importance of strengthening, maintaining, and supporting the parent-child relationship as the context of the child's development. All intensive family preservation programs seek to prevent the unnecessary interruption of this relationship as they work to prevent inappropriate out-of-home placement of children. Once placement is prevented, IFPS programs work to help families avoid the recurrence of the crises that led to the imminent risk of placement.

Intensive family preservation programs utilize a strength or growth model, a time-limited approach, an emphasis on the active participation of the client in the intervention, and stress the centrality of the relationship between the IFPS worker and the client. In addition, the focus upon the prevention of unnecessary out-of-home placement provides the "function" or purpose of the IFPS program. These tenets of IFPS programs have their roots in functional theory. Dore (1990) describes themes found in crisis intervention theory and in the ecological perspective that were initially articulated by functional theorists. Although functional theory has not yet been credited with contributing to the theory base of IFPS practice, it is important that functional theory be recognized as a part of the fundamental undergirding of family preservation practice. IFPS programs "embrace a collection of long-held and mostly ignored values, some new techniques, and some old techniques that are being re-emphasized" (Cole & Duva, 1990, p. 11). The functional perspective offers values and techniques, as well as theory, that have become integral to the provision of family preservation services.

References

Adnopoz, D. J., Grigsby, R. K. & Nagler, S. F. (1991). Multiproblem families and high-risk children and adolescents: Causes and management. In M. Lewis (Ed.), *Child and adolescent psychiatry: A comprehensive textbook*. Baltimore, MD: Williams & Wilkins.

Ainsworth, M. D. S. (1985). Attachments across the lifespan. *Bulletin of the New York Academy of Medicine, 61,* 792-812.

Ainsworth, M. D. S. (1989). Attachments beyond infancy. *American Psychologist, 44*(4), 709-716.

Bandura, A. (1977). *Social learning theory.* Englewood Cliffs, NJ: Prentice Hall.

Bank, S. P., & Kahn, M. D. (1982). *The sibling bond.* New York: Basic Books.

Barth, R. P. (1990). Theories guiding home-based intensive family preservation services. In J. K. Whittaker, J. Kinney, E. M. Tracy, & C. Booth (Eds.), *Reaching high-risk families: Intensive family preservation in human services*. Hawthorne, NY: Aldine de Gruyter.

Bowlby, J. (1969). *Attachment* (2nd ed). New York: Basic Books.

Bowlby, J. (1973). *Separation*. New York: Basic Books.

Bowlby, J. (1980). *Loss.* New York: Basic Books.

Bowlby, J. (1988). *A secure base.* New York: Basic Books.

Caplan, G. (1964). *Principles of preventive psychiatry.* New York: Basic Books.

Cole, E., & Duva, J. (1990). *Family preservation: An orientation for administrators and practitioners.* Washington, DC: Child Welfare League of America.

Dore, M. M. (1990). Functional theory: Its history and influence on contemporary social work practice. *Social Service Review, 64*(3), 358-374.

Florida Department of Health and Rehabilitative Services. (1990, December). Supplemental services: Intensive crisis counseling program (ICCP). In Florida Department of Health and Rehabilitative Services, *Outcome evaluation report.* Tallahassee: Author

Fraiberg, S. (1975). Ghosts in the nursery. *Journal of the American Academy of Child Psychiatry, 14,* 387-421.

Freud, A. (1965). *Normality and pathology in childhood: Assessments of development.* New York: International Universities Press.

Germain, C. B., & Gitterman, A. (1980). *The life model of social work practice.* New York: Columbia University Press.

Goldstein, J., Freud, A., & Solnit, A. J. (1973). *Beyond the best interests of the child.* New York: Free Press.

Kinney, J., Haapala, D. A., Booth, C., & Leavitt, S. (1990). The homebuilders model. In J. K. Whittaker, J. Kinney, E. M. Tracy, & C. Booth (Eds.), *Reaching high-risk families: Intensive family preservation in human services* (pp. 31-64). Hawthorne, NY: Aldine de Gruyter.

Lindemann, E. (1944). Symptomatology and management of acute grief. *American Journal of Psychiatry, 101,* 141-148.

Littner, N. (1967). *Some traumatic effects of separation and placement.* New York: Child Welfare League of America.

Minuchin, S. (1974). *Families and family therapy.* Cambridge, MA: Harvard University Press.

Nelson, K. E., Landsman, M. J., & Deutelbaum, W. (1990). Three models of family-centered placement prevention services. *Child Welfare, 69*(1), 3-21.

Parad, H. J., & Caplan, G. (1960). A framework for studying families in crisis. *Journal of Social Work, 5,* 3-15.

Polansky, N. A. (1986). There is nothing so practical as a good theory. *Child Welfare, 65*(1), 1-15.

Rzepnicki, T. L., Scheurman, J. R., & Littell, J. H. (1991). Issues in evaluating intensive family preservation services. In E. M. Tracy, D. A. Haapala, J. Kinney, & P. J. Pecora (Eds.), *Intensive family preservation services: An instructional sourcebook.* Cleveland, OH: Case Western Reserve University, Mandel School of Applied Social Sciences.

Spitz, R. (1945). Hospitalism: An inquiry into the genesis of psychiatric conditions in early childhood. *The Psychoanalytic Study of the Child, 1,* 53-74.

Smalley, R. E. (1967). *Theory for social work practice.* New York: Columbia University Press.

Smalley, R. E. (1971). Social casework: The functional approach. In *Encyclopedia of social work* (16th ed., Vol. 2). New York: National Association of Social Workers.

Stone, N. M., & Stone, S. F. (1983). The prediction of successful foster placement. *Social Casework, 64*(1), 11-17.

Taft, J. (1937). The relation of function to process. *Journal of Social Work Process, 1,* 1-18.

Thyer, B. A., & Maddox, M. K. (1988). Behavioral social work: results of a national survey on graduate curricula. *Psychological Reports, 63,* 239-242.

Thyer, B. A. (1991). Behavioral social work: It is not what you think. *Arete, 16*(2), 1-9.

University of Pennsylvania School of Social Work. (1990). *The Penn approach: An evolving philosophy of education for social work practice.* Philadelphia: Author.

3

Child Protective Services and Intensive Family Preservation

A Primary Relationship

ANN E. QUINN

The existence of a strong working relationship between an Intensive Family Preservation Services (IFPS) agency and a Child Protective Service (CPS) agency is paramount to a successful IFPS program. The potential for defensiveness and turf issues to arise are too great to ignore this requirement. Obviously, if this type of relationship does not exist prior to the development of the program then the first task is for the decision-making staff of each agency (at the local or regional level) to discuss the history of problems and problem resolution. Misconceptions and case-related problems that have lingered need to be aired in order to put them to rest. A working knowledge of both agencies' mandates, limitations, and expectations is imperative.

We were most fortunate in southeastern Connecticut to have already established a strong working relationship with the private host agency on which to build our IFPS program. Although we had not always agreed with one another concerning certain cases and situations, we had established a climate of mutual respect that allowed us to disagree and still work closely together.

The selection of our host agency for the IFPS program in southeastern Connecticut was strengthened by an already existing program of Family Violence services that mandated frequent worker and supervisor involvement with the family violence therapists and program administrators. This Family Violence program had a home visiting component that was utilized when it was clinically indicated or when it became necessary to engage a resistant or reluctant client.

The Family Violence program's mandate that the CPS worker and supervisor meet with the host agency staff and the referred family at the onset of the case and at periodic points during the case life not only strengthened the service offered to the family, but also provided an opportunity for the development of mutual respect between the public and private sectors. As each group saw the complexities and frustrations inherent in the jobs of the other, a mutual relationship developed that could withstand a difference of opinion or strategy and provided the base on which to work out any significant differences.

Commitment for a joint IFPS program needs to exist from the "top of the agency" (administration) on down to the direct service provider. If key regional administrators are enthusiastic, willing to be involved in the planning and implementation of the program, and they relate this to the staff below them, fewer problems will arise. One of the key issues for the development of the IFPS program at the host agency involves the request that CPS administrators be part of the interviewing process for the IFPS staff. This enables protective services to have not only a say in the decision-making process around the hiring of staff, but also allows the opportunity for both agencies to be clear with regard to the philosophy of the program as it is presented to those who are to become the implementors.

Critical Elements for a Strong Working Relationship

Once the IFPS staff is hired and trained it is important to take the time to allow the staff of each agency to get acquainted. A good technique to utilize in this process is to arrange for the IFPS staff to "shadow" protective service staff in the field for a period of time in order for them to understand the complexities of the public agency mandates and the limitation often placed upon them. Prior to this point, however, you may also want to invite some key protective service staff to IFPS trainings so that they have a sense of what the IFPS clinician will be doing with clients.

The second critical element in a strong IFPS program relates to the case review process. It is important that the relationship that has developed between staff is now nurtured and allowed to grow. The base for this growth is the communication about cases and the case decisions that need to be made. With a case life of only 6 to 8 weeks, meetings between the IFPS and CPS staff need to take place on a weekly basis in order for everyone to develop a sense of what is happening in the case and to ensure that the work proceeds "on target."

Initially, protective service administrative staff need to be involved in these case reviews. In addition to the worker and supervisor of the case, program supervisors should attend. The message is then clear that this is an important program. The meeting process is given credibility, and support for the kind of involvement that the worker and supervisor are making in the case is underscored. Although this is a large investment in time for any CPS agency to make, the benefits both in terms of the growth of the IFPS program and the clinical learning that takes in these meetings justifies the amount of time spent.

The Referral Process

An identified "gatekeeper" for agency referrals to the IFPS program is necessary. The IFPS agency should also identify a single person as a "point of contact" for referring cases. Ideally the gatekeeper should be at an administrative level, which will preclude the issue of conflict among peers vying for program services.

Initially, when there are multiple referrals needing IFP services and all other criteria are somewhat equal, attention should be given to seeing that as many workers and units have experience with the program as possible. Without conscious decision making in this area it is easy for units that have had a positive IFPS experience to monopolize the services while other units who have not had the experience might hold back. Like any new resource, an IFPS program can suffer from initially having too many referrals, followed by a period where there is a lack of referrals. Therefore, the gatekeeper needs to be someone involved in day-to-day case discussions so as to be able to suggest when an IFPS referral is appropriate or inappropriate.

There are several established criteria for making referrals to the IFPS program. A primary criterion is that one or more of the children in the family is at imminent risk of out-of-home placement. Second, the family, or at least one of the adult members of the family, agree to the service. Another issue to be addressed in the eligibility phase of the referral process relates to whether a less intrusive community resource could be utilized to keep this family intact, that is, a parent aide or family counseling. The resource has to be available to the family within an appropriate time frame.

The final criterion for eligibility for IFP services has to be the determination on the part of both agencies that the safety of the children is not being compromised by their remaining within the home with family preservation services.

The willingness of a family to accept family preservation intervention is related in large part to the presentation of the program made by the CPS worker to the family. All families have to be advised that placement of the child(ren) is being considered but that utilization of this special service could help to prevent that drastic action.

Initially CPS workers need help in developing a way in which to make the presentation to the family concerning the IFPS program. As they become more familiar with IFPS they are then able to use examples of services that other families were able to make use of in a supportive atmosphere.

The criterion that an IFPS referral is valid only when risk of placement is imminent can be problematic to anyone assigned gatekeeping duties, since it is partly a judgment call as to whether placement is in fact imminent. The potential for placement exists in any valid protective service case. To define the legitimacy of its imminence is part of the task of the gatekeeper. There are several reasons for utilizing this criterion. First and foremost, the limited availability of family preservation workers dictates the most judicious use of their skills. In addition to the economy issue, the use of crisis intervention theory suggests that families in crisis are more amenable to intervention while in the midst of the crisis. To match the family in crisis to the IFPS opening is not always a simple and easy task.

Engaging Families

Once the family has agreed to accept IFP services and meet with the clinician, the referral is officially made to the IFPS agency. At that point, contact by the family, preservation clinician, and the CPS worker is to take place within 24 hours.

During the initial phase of the IFPS process very few families openly reject the services offered. The CPS worker and the IFPS clinician use this opportunity to establish the roles and responsibilities of each agency. This process allows the family to begin to address the relationship of the IFPS clinician to CPS as well as the parameters of that relationship. In some cases the IFPS clinicians feel comfortable enough to begin—with the help of the family—defining the case goals and deciding on the services that need to be provided. In other case situations, particularly those where the CPS worker does not have the opportunity to establish much of a relationship, the IFPS clinician utilizes a later visit to address these issues.

IFPS clinicians must be clear with the family about what needs to be accomplished in order to avoid child placement in out-of-home care. They must also clearly identify the type of relationship they have with the protective service agency. As part of this disclosure, they must be clear with families that they are legally mandated reporters who must report suspected abuse and/or neglect to the authorities. This underscores the importance of trust and mutual respect between IFPS clinicians and CPS workers.

The IFPS clinician may provide or obtain a considerable range of services for a family. Direct intervention aimed at improving self-esteem, improving communication between family members, teaching anger control, teaching stress management, increasing frustration tolerance, and increasing the caregiver's repertoire of parenting skills are but a few of the areas most frequently addressed. Crisis intervention, advocacy, information and referral, case management, respite care, and homemaker services are provided by IFPS clinicians.

In the majority of cases it is necessary to identify the role of and appropriate tasks for CPS workers to perform in order to keep them involved once an IFPS referral has been made and treatment has commenced. A frequent criticism of in-home service providers is that the CPS worker "drops out" and is no longer meaningfully involved with the family once some other provider is working in the home. As a result of caseload size and pressures felt by protective service staff, this action is understandable but certainly not acceptable if the impact of intensive intervention is to be maximized. Therefore, it is important to discuss during the weekly progress meeting what the protective service worker has done and will continue to do with the referred family. In addition, a meeting scheduled halfway between the 6 to 8 weeks of IFPS intervention—with the family, the preservation clinician, and the CPS worker—is very important. This meeting will offer an opportunity for discussion about the progress or lack of progress made during the first half of intervention, and allow for redefinition of goals and objectives to be addressed with the family.

In the New London County region, referrals to the IFPS program come from treatment cases more often than from the initial intake process. With intake cases referred to the program, it becomes critical to identify immediately the treatment worker to be assigned and to introduce that individual to the family prior to or simultaneously with the preservation clinician. When this does not occur it becomes more difficult for the CPS treatment worker to establish a relationship with the family.

Effects of Intervention: What is Success?

Intensive family preservation intervention has a positive influence on family functioning in terms of upgrading parenting skills. Many families involved in our program learn new ways to parent their children more effectively. They learn new ways to view themselves and the significant others in their lives. Placement of children does not occur in a large majority of the cases. When placement is necessary it is often because the preservation clinician and the CPS worker determine together that significant risk to the child(ren) continues to exist.

Early on in our discussions the IFPS agency and CPS staff attempted to define how we would view success. Although we all agreed the central goal for family preservation was to avoid placement of children out of the home, we also verbalized the notion that placement of a child who needed to be out of the home because of the risk involved should not be automatically reviewed as a "failure."

The true value of family preservation intervention lies in what we learn about the family and the dynamics that led to the need for protective service intervention. Family dysfunction is not "cured" by such a short intensive service. Due to the nature of the intervention, the preservation clinician has the opportunity to observe family interaction and dynamics that might never be seen by the protective service staff. The clinician in a sense "learns the language of the family." This fact allows the clinician to aid the family in making referrals to ongoing longer term services that are the most appropriate given the individual problems that exist within the family. Acting as a bridge or conduit to these community services further enhances the likelihood that such services will be successful in the eyes of family members.

Given the nature of their mandate, protective service staff must first look at the risks or negative behavior that a family presents to a child's well-being. CPS workers tend to be more skillful at identifying a family's weaknesses rather than their strengths. As preservation staff and CPS staff work side by side, one senses that preservation staff are frequently able to accentuate the strengths that may have been overlooked by the protective service worker.

From an administrative point of view, the weekly case management meetings are beneficial in establishing an understanding of certain problems and procedures by CPS staff. The meetings provide the opportunity to discuss cases in depth, and both workers and supervisors are able to transfer what they learn from one case to another. Occasionally a worker or supervisor will express frustration and/or anger in these discussions. With time, the group becomes capable of dealing with the issues.

IFPS intervention has been used successfully in a variety of cases. In several family sexual abuse cases, the preservation clinician was able to be most helpful in dealing with the nonoffending spouse and in assisting that individual to work through the denial and anger phases. In one case the offender was allowed to return to the home while in treatment because the other parent was determined to be capable of protecting and supporting the child. In another case enough support was provided by the clinician to allow the mother to successfully terminate a destructive relationship.

Other Uses for IFPS

We have experimented quite successfully with the use of IFP services in maintaining reunification cases and in the prevention of adoption disruption. In preventing reunification cases from resulting in the replacement of the child, the preservation clinician can help the family first to anticipate and then to begin to deal successfully with the problems presented. Thus the family and child are able to remain together.

In cases of potential adoption disruption, the issue for child welfare workers is to decide whether it is a placement that should be terminated or whether extra emergency efforts should be expended to get the family past the crisis and maintain the placement. The use of a preservation clinician in this kind of situation provides the opportunity to resolve this issue.

It is exciting to speculate that future family preservation services might be available to prevent foster home placements from disrupting.

One type of case that IFPS intervention seems to serve less successfully is long-term chronic neglecting families. Families identified as chronically neglectful seem to have the least success with IFPS intervention. As we looked at our mutual experiences with these families, it becomes evident that they seem less able to take what was taught during a current crisis and apply what they learned to the next crisis. The short-term nature of intensive intervention does not seem to lend itself to such families who appear to need lifelong intervention.

Although many families seem to be positively affected by IFPS intervention, a majority of them also continue to need further home-based services at a less intensive level. The creation of a position by our IFPS host agency for a clinician who could carry as many as 10 cases while still being able to make home visits does seem to fill this gap. This individual continues the work done by the preservation clinician and hopefully continues to move this type of family to a place where less intensive community services can meet the needs of the family.

Results

The basic demographics of cases referred during the first year of the IFPS program in Region III showed that 42 families—involving 99 children—were referred for these services. The average age of the children referred was 7 years and the average age of the adults was 31 years. The majority of cases referred involved physical abuse (34%) and severe neglect (32%). Of the children served, 31% had previously been placed in out-of-home care during the past 5 years. Fifty-three percent of the families were single parent households and 65% of the total families served were receiving public assistance.

As further experience is obtained in the use of IFPS intervention, other areas should be addressed through data collection and research. These include, but are not limited to, looking at the difference between cases referred at the intake stage and those already assigned treatment workers, an assessment of the expectations of IFPS intervention in severe chronic neglect cases, and looking at whether to extend the time period of intervention with neglecting families to determine if this would allow for greater impact on family change. Another area to be explored relates to what differences exist between IFPS programs managed and operated by child protective service agencies themselves and those contracted out to private agencies.

Intensive family preservation involves significant investment both in time and money. In many ways, this is a wise investment as we are investing in our future. Children and families at risk need this type of investment in order to develop successfully as productive citizens.

PART II

Evolving Practice Models

4

Clinician-Support Worker Teams in Family Preservation

Are Two Heads Better Than One?

CHARLES R. SOULÉ
KAARINA MASSARENE
KATHLEEN ABATE

Over the past 10 years, a variety of program models have been developed to deliver intensive family preservation services in the home. Nelson, Landesman, and Deutelbaum (1990) surveyed 11 programs in different parts of the country and found that these programs share a common belief that families should be the focus of services, but organize the delivery of their services quite differently. Two key differences they found were the number and the type of staff used to provide services. In this chapter, we draw upon our own experience to discuss the consequences of two different staffing models currently employed in family preservation work: (a) single-clinician interventions, in which

AUTHORS' NOTE: We would like to acknowledge the assistance and support of both present and former colleagues at the Family Support Service, including Jean Adnopoz, R. Kevin Grigsby, Steven F. Nagler, and Tracy Washington. In particular, we wish to thank Maggie Conley, Annie Ford, and Cathy Gertsch, the family support workers who share so much of themselves in this work.

Inquiries regarding this chapter should be sent to Charles R. Soulé, Yale Child Study Center, Family Support Service, 230 South Frontage Road, P.O. Box 3333, New Haven, CT 06510-8009.

all services are provided by a master's-level or doctoral-level child and family clinician; and (b) clinician-support worker team interventions, where clinicians work along with agency-trained family support workers. Our focus in this chapter is clinical and experiential; we discuss the impact of each staffing pattern on the relationships that develop between families and preservation workers, on the course of the work done to prevent placements, and on the work experience of the clinicians and support workers.

Staffing Models in Family Preservation

In a discussion of many different types of home-visiting services for children and families, Wasik, Bryant, and Lyons (1990) noted that these services have a long history of employing both professional and lay workers (referred to hereafter as support workers). Three related factors tend to determine which type of workers are employed: (a) the specific program goals and objectives, (b) the level of training and expertise believed to be necessary to meet a program's goals and objectives, and (c) the presence or absence of a commitment to employ workers from the same communities or backgrounds as the families being served. Professionals are usually the sole providers of services that require specific training or expertise (e.g. visiting nurses). Conversely, support workers are often the providers in agencies that see a similarity in background between workers and families as likely to render their services more effective. A third, frequent alternative is to pair professionals with support workers when effective services require both formal training and the enhanced sensitivity and rapport that community workers can provide.

Both single clinicians and teams have been employed in family preservation programs. However, the most well-known model nationally is the Homebuilders program, which relies upon single, professional clinicians to provide services. Kinney, Haapala, Booth, and Leavitt (1990) advance several arguments in support of single-clinician interventions. They note that: (a) a single clinician must take responsibility for all family members, and is less likely to ally with individual members or family subsystems in ways that subvert the work with a family; (b) it is usually easier and less invasive for families to accept and engage with one rather than two workers; (c) families often develop more rapport with workers who provide concrete as well as therapeutic services, thereby enhancing the effectiveness of both types of interventions; (d) the necessary communication and coordination between team members is time-consuming and may not be cost-effective in short-term, intensive interventions; and (e) the presence of two workers introduces potential complications from problematic co-worker relationships, while diluting accountability.

In contrast to the Homebuilders model, family preservation programs have developed in a number of states using two providers to staff their cases. In some of these programs, both workers are professional clinicians, whereas in other programs, professional clinicians are paired with support workers. In this chapter we limit our discussion to single-clinician models and teams that mix professional clinicians and support workers. Lloyd, Bryce, and Schulze (1984) cite several advantages inherent in clinician-support worker team interventions. They argue that: (a) team members can lend each other crucial support in what are often highly charged situations or severely dysfunctional families; (b) the use of teams doubles therapeutic expertise and objectivity, lessening the likelihood that workers may become enmeshed in dysfunctional family dynamics; (c) service continuity can be maintained when one worker on a team is temporarily unavailable; (d) the presence of two workers allows for more flexibility in therapeutic roles, and in working with different individuals or subsystems within a family; and (e) support workers are more likely to share common backgrounds with families, and are thus more able to develop rapport with families who will not use professional services or who have negative histories with such services.

Currently, there does not exist sufficient empirical evidence to indicate that either single clinicians or clinician-support worker teams are more effective in delivering family preservation services. Each of the rationales outlined above is theoretically and experientially valid, that is, each reflects some aspect of the underlying theories and of the practical experience of family preservationists. In our view, the key question is not whether one or the other model has an overall advantage in family preservation work. Instead, the existence of competing models and rationales confirms our own experience that the course of a family preservation intervention is influenced heavily by how the intervention is staffed. If we can understand the different consequences of one or the other model (upon a family and upon the work accomplished), we may be able to answer a more finely tuned question: For which families, and/or for what types of placement issues is one or the other model more appropriate?

Utilizing Both Service Models Within One Program

In order to look at the differences that flow from single-clinician and clinician-support worker team interventions, we draw upon our experience as clinicians who work in both models. The work we describe was performed at the Family Support Service (FSS), a program of the Yale Child Study Center. FSS was founded in 1985, through a grant from the Edna McConnell Clark Foundation. FSS currently makes available four home-based family preservation programs, each targeted at separate at-risk populations of children. The program described in this chapter is the Intensive Family Preservation (IFP) program, which is funded by the Connecticut Department of Children and Youth Services (DCYS), the comprehensive state agency for children. The IFP program seeks to maintain abused and/or neglected children with their biological parents or other natural caretakers, when it is in the best interests of children to remain with those caretakers.

Initially, clinician-support worker teams provided all services in the IFP program. Beginning in 1990, the program expanded to serve families with two staffing models: the original clinician-support worker teams, and single clinicians. During the first year in which both models operated (FY 1990-1991), clinicians worked in either one or the other model. In order to facilitate an evaluation of which families might be best served by single clinicians or by teams, families were assigned to one or the other model based solely on whether a single clinician or team clinician was next available to provide services. At the start of the second year in which both models operated (FY 1991-1992), clinicians were assigned to carry cases in both models, creating a unique opportunity to compare work done singly and in teams. At this point, families continue to be assigned to one or the other model on a case-available basis.

The clinicians working in the IFP program are master's-level social workers and doctoral-level clinical psychologists, with training in child and family issues. The support workers, known at FSS as family support workers, are recruited from the communities we serve, and typically have strong life experience as parents, as formal and informal helpers, and as active community members (Grigsby & Gertsch, 1989). Both clinicians and family support workers serve four families at a time. Currently, clinicians carry three cases with family support workers, and carry the fourth case alone. Clinicians and support workers are assigned to each case as they become available, so that over the course of time, each clinician is able to work with every support worker in the program. Families receive services for 8 to 12 weeks, with an average of three visits per week.

In team interventions, roles between clinicians and family support workers are flexible. Clinicians are responsible for the overall direction of the case, but both members of the team participate in the assessment of family needs, the development of treatment or service plans, and the delivery of agreed-upon services. In particular, both clinicians and support workers share responsibility for providing concrete services to families. Depending upon the specific placement issues in a family, and which member of the team is best able to establish a close working relationship with individual family members, either or both may engage in parent guidance and education, brief individual and family treatments, and linkage and advocacy with other agencies. Throughout an intervention, team members exchange information and clinical impressions that are used to evaluate the progress made to date, and to modify a case plan or guide further interventions toward case goals (Grigsby & Gertsch, 1989; Vitulano, Nagler, Adnopoz, & Grigsby, 1990).

All children served by the IFP program are referred by state child protective services when at imminent risk of placement due to abuse or neglect. The program serves a wide geographic area that includes inner-city, working-class, and more affluent suburban communities. In the 1990-1991 fiscal year, the program served 189 children in 81 families. Two-thirds (120 children in 56 families, or 63% of the children) were served in the team model, and one-third (56 children in 25 families, or 37% of the children) were seen by single clinicians. Infants and very young children predominated: 45% of children were 5 years of age or younger, 35% were between 6 and 10 years, and 20% were between 11 and 17 years. Children from minority ethnic communities also predominated: 48% were African American, 31% were Caucasian, 14% were Hispanic, and 6% were biracial. Three quarters (75%) of the children came from single-parent households, and from families receiving state income assistance. The majority of children (58%) were referred for neglect, 18% were referred for physical and/or sexual abuse, 7% were referred after their parents requested that they be removed from the home, and 17% were referred for other reasons.

Doubling Practical and Therapeutic Resources

One of the immediately apparent consequences of teaming family preservation cases is that the amount of practical and therapeutic resources potentially available to a family doubles. The great majority of the families we serve are experiencing multiple stressors, including: extreme poverty, violence both within their communities and within their home, past or current substance abuse, chronic illness, the collapse or absence of family or other natural support networks, inexperienced and very young single parents, and responsibility for several very young children. A typical list of concrete service needs for children in a single family can include: food; housing; entitlements; utilities; specialized medical treatments, educational programs, or developmental therapies; and legal services.

These concrete stressors may increase parents' dependency upon outside providers, while at the same time engendering in them distrust and lessening their likelihood to enter into effective relationships with helpers. Successful interventions in these situations require that providers invest substantial time and effort in both developing a strong working relationship with parents and in securing needed assistance from other agencies. The demands upon a single clinician can be nearly overwhelming. The following case example illustrates this point:

Jay, age 7, Tina, age 2, and Tom, age 1, reside with their mother, Dee, age 25. The children's father, Pete, lives in the house intermittently. Dee was referred to child protective services (CPS) by her grandmother, who was concerned that Dee regularly left the children unsupervised while bingeing on cocaine and alcohol. Dee acknowledged chronic drug use and stated that, as a consequence, she was not providing adequate physical or emotional care for her children. Tina seemed unusually susceptible to serious respiratory infections and appeared developmentally delayed. Jay, although only 7, appeared parentified, taking care of his siblings in his mother's absence and denying the chronic domestic violence that both parents reported.

On intake, Dee requested inpatient drug treatment. Dee had no phone or access to one, and needed assistance with contacting programs and transportation to admission interviews. Considerable emotional support was required to walk Dee through the drug treatment selection and intake process.

Once drug treatment was secured, further efforts were required to assist Dee in making child-care arrangements with members of her extended family. This also necessitated arrangements to transfer AFDC payments temporarily and to transfer temporary guardianship of the children, both time-consuming and emotionally charged processes.

Other services included arrangements for routine medical care for all three children, as well as referrals for developmental assessments and appropriate remediation programs for Tina. The clinician also made several emergency visits to deal with violence between Dee and Pete, and to provide transportation to a local hospital emergency room following an accidental injury to the 1-year-old. In addition, Dee was assisted with telephone service, utilities, and emergency food.

The therapeutic focus addressed marital issues through extended family counseling sessions that dealt with both parents' substance abuse, violent behavior, and their difficulties in meeting their children's physical, developmental, and emotional needs. Efforts were made to engage both parents in long-term outpatient treatments for substance abuse and marital conflict.

A foster care placement was averted for these three children, and at the case closing, the family situation was somewhat more stable, with intermittent participation by Dee in outpatient drug treatment groups, appropriate services in place for the children, and improved secure housing.

Given the chronic pattern of crises in this family, and the multiplicity of services needed, it was necessary for the single clinician to extend her service to 15 weeks. The intensity and the greater duration of services made it difficult for this family to terminate with the family preservation clinician, and difficult for them to continue with other longer term services.

A second example illustrates the advantages of team staffing for a family with a similar high number of concrete service needs:

Tory, age 4, Frankie, age 3, Ben, age 2, and Vonda, age 2 weeks, reside with their mother, Willie, age 21. The father of the two younger children is in the household, but is alleged to use and deal drugs. CPS became active in the family due to medical neglect of Frankie and Ben. Neither Frankie nor Ben had received routine checkups and immunizations, and Ben was unable to walk due to poor muscle tone in his feet. He had been previously referred for physical therapy, but Willie had not taken Ben for this treatment. There were also allegations that drug trafficking was occurring regularly in the family home.

Upon intake, the first issue addressed was the need to secure Medicaid coverage for Frankie, Ben, and Vonda, something Willie had never arranged. Beyond this, routine medical care and physical therapy were secured for Frankie and Ben, as well as treatment for an infection in both Willie and her newborn, Vonda. Willie was also assisted in obtaining a tubal ligation, which she had requested. Attempts were made to reconnect Willie with a drug treatment group she had previously attended, as well as to assist her with obtaining utilities, appliances, regular transportation to medical appointments, and child care.

The therapeutic work with Willie focused on her apparent strong attachment to her children, and the ways in which her depression and substance abuse impaired her ability to meet their needs consistently. This work, as well as the numerous concrete services engaged, was performed by both the clinician and family support worker. Tasks were divided solely on the basis of each worker's availability, and much of the therapeutic relationship with Willie was developed and fostered while each worker provided concrete services.

Team members complemented each other's strengths and skills; the clinician was able to provide a clinical understanding of Willie's stressors and her intrapsychic and interpersonal functioning, while the family support worker was adept at accessing resources and connecting with known and trusted providers in other systems. Together they were able to share perspectives and ego strengths and to model cooperative problem solving and goal setting.

In many families nearly every concrete service need is either tied to an unmet emotional or psychological need, or stimulates negative feelings and beliefs in family members. For example, a variety of concerns can inhibit parents from seeking available services or entitlements, such as concerns that they may appear ignorant, that they may be judged negatively by service providers, and that they may call attention to themselves and thereby incur further state sanctions. Other parents may expect little benefit from seeking help, and may have strong feelings against placing themselves in a dependent position vis-à-vis service agencies and professionals. In order to assist a family to identify and use available resources, workers must first understand and address the individual meaning of such services to parents. In families with multiple problems, the therapeutic work required in addition to concrete services can be more easily provided when two workers are present.

Even in families where the placement prevention work is more exclusively therapeutic, team staffing increases the number of roles and interventions that can be used to serve a family. This is especially important in cases where there are multiple family members who must be engaged, or in situations where family members are better able to develop a relationship with one or another worker. For example, a common treatment plan when working with large, highly conflicted families is to support the changes accomplished in family sessions through additional work with individual family members and subsystems. The availability of two workers is invaluable in such situations, as illustrated by another case example.

Samuel, age 16, and his sister, Rose, age 15, were referred for preservation services when being discharged from psychiatric hospitalizations. Both teens had lived at home with their mother, Maria, and their brother, Ricky, age 12. Maria's primary language is Spanish, but all three children are fully bilingual. Samuel had been hospitalized after a severe family conflict in which he damaged furnishings and made homicidal threats against his stepfather, Victor. Rose had been hospitalized 2 weeks later, after a serious suicide attempt. These events were precipitated by conflict in the family regarding Victor, who had a 7-year history of verbally harassing Rose with explicit sexual comments and suggestions. Following Rose's suicide attempt, Maria had reluctantly asked Victor to leave the family home. However, given continued conflict between Maria and her children, hospital staff had recommended that Samuel and Rose be placed in foster homes.

Rose returned home from the hospital when preservation services began, but Samuel was transferred to the adolescent unit of a state psychiatric hospital, due to continued concerns about his suicidal and homicidal ideation. The family preservation team consisted of a male clinician and a female family support worker. The team began by jointly conducting scheduled and emergency family sessions to address the conflicts between Rose and her mother. The clinician took the lead in these meetings, conducting them in Spanish for Maria's sake, and focused on the sources and possible resolutions of conflict between Maria and Rose. The family support worker supported this work in individual sessions with Rose.

The mother-daughter relationship improved significantly over two or three sessions, but conflict then erupted between Rose and Ricky, leading to abrupt and explosive exits from family meetings and a serious incident of violence between the two siblings. The clinician met with the family in a weekend session to defuse the immediate conflict. The clinician then met individually with Ricky, while the family support worker met individually with Rose. In subsequent family meetings, the level of conflict between Rose and Ricky decreased and then disappeared.

The importance of team staffing became apparent again in subsequent family meetings that took place at the hospital in order to include Samuel. Repeating the earlier pattern with Maria and Rose, these meetings soon stalemated over Maria's angry rejection of Samuel. This occurred after Samuel asked that he not return home immediately after discharge, but move to a foster home for some period of time. Given Samuel's history and the potential for continued conflict, foster care with an ongoing family treatment and a plan for eventual reunification seemed in Samuel's best interests.

At this point the clinician attempted to meet individually with Maria, who agreed, but then canceled two appointments. The family support worker then offered to meet with Maria and Maria's aunt, who could translate. Maria again attempted to cancel at the last moment, but the presence of her aunt seemed to tip the balance in favor of the meeting. Maria asked to go out to breakfast, an activity the family support worker used in her meetings with Maria's daughters. The family support worker used her common experience as a single parent of adolescents to engage Maria and to offer Maria support for the difficulty of her role. Maria responded very positively, and requested further meetings.

Family Support Worker-Client Relationships

In the last case example the family support worker was in a position to engage an angry and fearful parent, because she could speak from her own life experience to create a bond of understanding and support. In some instances the family support workers have access to relationships with clients different from what is available to even the most skillful clinician. Along these lines, Grigsby and Gertsch (1989) suggest that many families experience a special sense of affiliation with support workers. Our experience suggests two reasons why this is so. The first is that there is often a greater match in personal and sociocultural background between clients and family support workers than between clients and clinicians. This is especially true in the ethnically diverse, low-income, and working-class communities that we serve most frequently. Clients immediately perceive this difference in match and as a consequence they often respond quickly and positively to the family support worker.

The ethnic or racial barriers between clinicians and clients can be reduced by hiring diverse professional staff. By definition, however, clinicians of whatever ethnic background differ in class and education from low-income or working-class clients. This is so even in cases where clinicians may have similar personal or family histories; more important, our clients perceive it to be so when they work with clinicians. The differences in education, occupation, and income mean that clinicians usually do not have personal knowledge of the social and environmental stressors facing clients. In contrast, family support workers typically have experiences in their own adult histories similar to those of many clients whom they serve. Furthermore, family support workers often live in the same communities as clients, bringing to their work a familiarity with the informal as well as formal neighborhood resources, and a street savvy and interpersonal style that clients recognize as their own.

A second factor also enables support workers to engage families in ways that are different from the relationships created with clinicians. Although both clinicians and support workers are formal helpers, clinicians' training and professional role creates greater distance between themselves and clients. To be effective, family support workers must also operate within clear boundaries, but their roles allow clients more space to perceive similarities, to identify with the worker, and to model their decisions and behavior after what a worker demonstrates or suggests. It is not unusual, for example, for families to share some common social connection (e.g., schools, local churches, etc.) with support workers. Even when this is not so, clients are freer to perceive family support workers as peers or elders in their own communities who have achieved more success in their lives. Clinicians, on the other hand, are nearly always seen as others who have enjoyed more advantages, or who have access to power and authority foreign to the local community or family. As a consequence, information or suggestions presented by a clinician often has a very different connotation than when given by a family support worker. These points are illustrated in the following case example:

Tasha, 12, had been living for 8 months in a preadoptive foster home. She had left her biological parents' home 3 years earlier, after an incident of physical abuse. She and her foster mother were referred for preservation services after Tasha reported that she had been physically abused by a friend of her adopting foster mother. Tasha was moved to a second foster home, but CPS workers questioned the report of abuse, and felt strongly that it reflected anxiety and ambivalence regarding the pending adoption. They requested assistance in returning Tasha to what they believed could be a successful and positive permanent home.

At the initial meeting, Tasha appeared anxious, mistrustful, and reluctant to engage. However, the family support worker assigned to the case was familiar with Tasha's community and school, and was herself the mother of a 14-year-old girl whom Tasha knew and liked. This personal connection created a basis for both workers in the team to engage Tasha. The clinician and support worker proceeded to meet separately with Tasha. The clinician conducted a more formal assessment, and took primary responsibility for meeting with the foster mother and Tasha's biological family (with whom she still had contact—a source of distress to the foster mother).

As a parent in her community, the family support worker was able to develop a relationship with Tasha from which she could provide the team with her observations and insights, often based upon direct information from Tasha. Together, the team pooled their information and understanding to guide the intervention and to formulate an appropriate plan in Tasha's best interests.

The Impact of Teamwork on Family Preservation Interventions

The previous sections have discussed the advantages of adding another provider, the family support worker, in family preservation cases. The final section of this chapter addresses another question: In what ways does operating as a team influence how both the family and the workers experience the intervention? For families, the opportunity to work with a collaborative team has consequences that go beyond the doubling of resources and the introduction of another worker who is seen as more like the family. For workers, the opportunity to collaborate brings additional challenges, but also additional support and a qualitatively different stance or role in the family. The impact on how both families and workers experience the intervention has consequences that influence outcome.

From the family perspective, receiving services from an effective team can communicate that cooperation, a reasonable division of tasks and roles, and joint responsibility for outcomes are all feasible. Many of the families we serve have little experience of effective collaboration between two adults. In these families only one parent is actually present, or the second parent is present but uncommitted to family tasks, or the parents actively undermine and oppose each other. The family preservation team demonstrates that it is possible for two adults to define common goals and pursue them in a way that the legitimate needs of each individual are met.

The presence of a team also appears to foster positive relationships between families and workers, while acting to defuse the intensity of attachments that family members sometimes form with a single worker. While positive relationships with workers are crucial to increase parents' self-esteem and their motivation to remedy family problems, the attendant risk in creating these relationships is that family members will transfer their needs for regard and care onto workers in ways that exceed what the workers can legitimately provide. An overly developed bond to a worker often becomes apparent when family members seem to generate new crises as the worker leaves the family following a successful intervention. The presence of two workers tackling different family needs focuses greater attention on the specific goals that bring the team into the family. This steady emphasis on the purpose of the intervention can ease difficulties when closing a case, as well as provide more opportunities for appropriate follow-up activities.

A common concern in team staffing of any intervention is that it presents both clients and workers with opportunities for "splitting" (i.e., viewing one individual as entirely positive, and another as entirely negative). This is unavoidable; the key question in our view is not how to prevent instances of splitting, but how to contain their destructive potential while using them to gain further understanding of a family and to shape future interventions. This requires two elements: (a) a commitment from both workers to deal directly and honestly with any differences that emerge between them regarding the course of events, the character or actions of family members, and the best possible course for subsequent work; and (b) adequate opportunities for team supervision or case consultation to uncover and explore splitting by family members and/or between the workers.

Strategies for managing splitting are similar to those employed to deal with any strong positive or negative reactions between family members and workers. In our experience, team members feel safest to reveal and explore team differences or negative reactions from family members when supervisors and other program staff view these events as helpful sources of information, either about the general issues and modes of operating within a family, or about workers' own values and biases (or both). In either case, the most useful stance is one that is nonjudgmental but that emphasizes the importance of uncovering and understanding the source of strong emotional reactions either in the family or in workers.

The additional investment of time and effort required to coordinate and supervise teamwork can pay off handsomely when one considers the impact that successful collaboration has on the workers' own experience of their work. As noted by other authors, an immediate benefit is the mutual support and expertise that two workers can provide to each other. The issues present in many of the families referred for preservation services are complex, contradictory, and demanding. The level of organization and resources within a family may be extremely low or even chaotic, and the amount of time and emotional investment required periodically feels overwhelming to preservation workers. Team members routinely develop a sense of shared experience with a family that allows them to offer each other support and validation for the stress and emotional investment that is involved in serving a family.

In particular, workers derive a tremendous degree of support and confidence from the independent observations of another worker who has direct knowledge of the family. These second observations can confirm the worker's own perceptions, refine them with further information or a slightly different perspective, or challenge the worker to examine the sources of his or her own perceptions and assessments. In any of these cases, the other worker's observations provide a baseline against which it is possible to test the soundness and objectivity of one's own judgments. This ongoing dual assessment grounds each worker in a way that complements and expands what an outside supervisor can provide. As a consequence, team members conduct their work with a greater degree of assurance that they are proceeding in ways that will be useful to a family.

From the worker's perspective, working in a team also emphasizes helpful boundaries between themselves and families, and promotes a clearer definition of their role. Beginning a family preservation intervention often means entering a very powerful, if sometimes dysfunctional, family system. The pressures upon workers to join the system in ways that do not challenge existing patterns (or that replicate them) are subtle but enormous. In especially troubled situations, workers often experience a sense of being incorporated or even ingested by the family. The worker's tool in managing these dynamics is to maintain and represent a system that is external to the family, but that seeks to enter the family temporarily and work alongside its members. This external system is represented by the worker's agency, co-workers, other workers, and other agencies that are mobilizing to provide needed services.

In single-clinician interventions, clinicians must mentally represent the outside world to themselves, and behaviorally represent that world to family members in every contact with the family. Staffing a family preservation intervention with a team embodies the notion of an outside system seeking to ally with a family; in a sense, each team worker physically brings her or his system along in every joint contact with a family. In case consultation meetings, we have developed a metaphor to compare the clinician's experience of a family in single-clinician and team interventions. In single-clinician interventions, it is as if the clinician were a free, single electron and the family a complete atom—the clinician experiences a tremendous pull from the family to join their system. In team interventions, the clinician and family support worker constitute their own complete system that enters the family temporarily as a subsystem with a defined purpose, but that can maintain its own boundaries and function more easily than might be the case for a single clinician.

Staffing a family preservation intervention with a team allows preservation workers to experience themselves as more appropriately separate from families, better enables them to perceive and work with family resistance to change, and allows them to focus more consistently and effectively on the goals of the intervention. This is especially critical in situations where family members' psychological needs and dysfunctional coping strategies are as great as their concrete needs. In these cases, the presence of two workers in a family checks the workers' unconscious impulses to meet family needs and demands in ways that mimic or repeat codependent patterns in the family itself.

Matching Models to Families

When compared to single-clinician models, our experience suggests that the use of clinician-family support worker teams influences the course of family preservation work in three major areas. First, the teams can potentially double the amount of treatment, advocacy, and concrete services available to families to avert placement of their children. Second, family support workers bring a perspective that is often closer to the experience of the families receiving services; are often able to engage more quickly or completely with families; and offer families a worker with whom they may more readily identify, or from whom they may more easily accept support and guidance. Third, teams can create a different process in working with families—they model effective cooperation, they defuse overattachments or overdependent relationships with workers, they provide workers with mutual support for difficult work, and they enhance workers' abilities to maintain helpful boundaries and a consistent focus on the goals of the intervention.

These advantages are perhaps most pronounced when serving families with the characteristics and presenting problems most commonly seen in our program. This may include families from ethnically and racially diverse communities, where services staffed solely by professionals have been historically underused and where early terminations or incomplete treatments are common in traditional service settings. It may also include families presenting with multiple and severe external stressors, especially poverty, social isolation, and dangerous living conditions. Finally, it may include single-parent families, families with very youthful parents and children, and families where parental substance abuse and/or neglect are often the issues placing children at risk of losing their family.

As a field, family preservation appears to be moving toward a flowering of different service models, tailored to local needs and to different types of families who present different placement issues and risks. Along these lines, the value of clinician-support worker teams has been recognized as one such innovation in a variety of preservation programs across the country (Nelson et al., 1990). Recently, the state of Florida initiated pilot family preservation projects using support workers paired with clinicians in two districts of the state (Florida Department of Health, 1990). This follows a 10-year history of providing family preservation services with single clinicians.

In conclusion, we would suggest that no single model of staffing is a panacea in work that is by definition highly stressful and demanding of both workers and families. It is important to note that our experience with both single-clinician and team staffing confirms the evidence of others that both models can be highly effective means for intervening with families where traditional, agency-based services seem insufficient to prevent out-of-home placement of children. We can also easily imagine situations or families in which a single worker may be preferable (e.g., parents who show extreme difficulty in engaging any outside worker or service). When we encounter such situations, we do not hesitate to reduce the direct involvement of one member of the team, or to remove a worker if need be. In our view, the challenge in each family preservation intervention is to assess carefully and continuously the impact that our ways of working have upon a family, and to tailor our models and services to meet the unique needs of each individual and family we encounter.

References

Florida Department of Health and Rehabilitative Services. (1990, December). *Outcome evaluation report*. Tallahassee: Author.

Grigsby, R. K., & Gertsch, C. (1989, October). *The family support worker: A distinct category of service provider*. Paper presented at the annual meeting of the National Association of Social Workers, San Francisco.

Kinney, J., Haapala, D. A., Booth, C., & Leavitt, S. (1990). The homebuilders model. In J. K. Whittaker, J. Kinney, E. M. Tracy, & C. Booth (Eds.), *Reaching high-risk families: Intensive family preservation in human services* (pp. 31-64). Hawthorne, NY: Aldine de Gruyter.

Lloyd, J. C., Bryce, M. E., & Schulze, L. (1984). *Placement prevention and family reunification: A handbook for the family-centered service practitioner*. Oakdale: University of Iowa, School of Social Work, National Resource Center on Family Based Services.

Nelson, K. E., Landesman, M. T., & Deutelbaum, W. (1990). Three models of family-centered placement prevention services. *Child Welfare, 69*, 3-21.

Vitulano, L. A., Nagler, S. F., Adnopoz, D. J., & Grigsby, R. K. (1990). Preventing out-of-home placement for high-risk children. *Yale Journal of Biology and Medicine, 63*, 285-291.

Wasik, B. H., Bryant, D. M., & Lyons, C. L. (1990). *Home visiting: Procedures for helping families*. Newbury Park, CA: Sage.

5

Evolving Family Preservation Services

The Florida Experience

RICHARD SCHAFER
SANDRA D. ERICKSON

As early as the 1930s, parts of Florida were offering child welfare services to a limited population. By 1935, services had expanded to 6 of 67 counties as a result of a $23,000 demonstration project. Over the next 55 years, services were legislatively mandated by federal and state statute to the extent that more than 7,000 staff statewide administer and provide services to an at-risk child population estimated to be 3,058,988 in fiscal year 1990-1991.

Background

Through the 1960s, services for children in the physical custody of the department and for those living in their own homes were scarce, inadequately funded even for that time, and poorly coordinated. By 1971, the Florida Legislature revised the state's statutes mandating the reporting of child abuse and neglect and providing for the investigation and treatment of abuse and neglect. This was the start of an effort to develop a uniform, comprehensive protective services program that would dovetail with existing programs offered in each county to dependent children. Specifically, the services for dependent children would include:

1. investigation of all complaints of neglect, abuse, abandonment, and alleged dependency;
2. initiation of necessary court action to ensure protection of children believed to be dependent;
3. preparation of and submission to the court of reports of findings and recommendations for handling on behalf of dependent children;
4. counseling and casework services for parents and relatives responsible for dependent and alleged to be dependent children in an attempt to stimulate changes necessary to ameliorate conditions in the home;
5. supervision of dependent children in their own or relatives' home;
6. removal and placement in family emergency shelters of children found in hazardous situations; and
7. placement in foster homes of children whose best interests demand that they be separated from their own families.

Until 1975, status offenses (running away, truancy, and beyond parental control) were considered delinquent behaviors. Legislation passed that year decriminalized these offenses and required the department to treat these children as dependent. Florida redirected its efforts to expedite permanency planning for its foster children and by 1981 implemented the federal mandate to provide preventive services to children and their families that would prevent unnecessary removal of children from their homes.

The latter part of the seventies and early eighties also produced other significant legislation in the interest of children. This legislation included:

1976: The passage of the Judicial Review of Foster Care Act to ensure a permanent family for children in foster care through periodic judicial reviews and adoption subsidy legislation that facilitated adoption of special needs children.

1978: Sufficient state funds were appropriated to increase adoption staff 300% and to purchase adoption placement services from private adoption agencies. Departmental restructuring of foster care was initiated to facilitate adoption of special needs children. A pilot of one Child Protection Team in Jacksonville was created to ensure a systematic approach in working with children and families at risk by providing joint staffings, planning, and management of cases to ensure integration and coordination of services.

1980: Judicial review requirements were expanded to include all public and private agencies that were providing care for children in order to expedite permanent placement through a return home or by adoption. A Guardian Ad Litem Project was created that mandated appointment of guardians to advocate for the best interest of children in abuse and neglect court proceedings.

1981-1982: Major initiatives were designed to impact on the number of children entering foster care by preventing removals from the home. These initiatives included: (a) funding of support services including individual and family counseling, parent effectiveness training, homemaker service, and two pilot intensive in-home services programs later called Intensive Crisis Counseling; (b) increased protective supervision staffing; and (c) 1.1 million dollars was appropriated to fund child abuse and neglect prevention projects in all 11 departmental districts statewide.

These initiatives were even more significant considering that major federal funding was being cut back at a time when most states were reporting increases in child abuse and neglect cases, including more serious types of maltreatment such as sexual abuse and deaths due to abuse. More than one half of all the states reported reductions in staff and service dollars. Florida was one of only three states that experienced an increase in availability of services for this group of abused and neglected children and their families.[1]

The Florida Legislature established funding priorities that emphasized prevention and treatment of child abuse and neglect at a time of decreasing state and federal dollars. Oversight committees of the Department of Health and Rehabilitative Services and the Criminal Justice Subcommittee on Appropriations for the Florida House of Representatives reported a rapid increase in known child abuse and neglect. Table 5.1 clearly shows the growth in abuse and neglect reports and the rising average daily foster care population from 1972 to the present.

Dramatic increases can be seen in fiscal year 1971-1972, the first full year that legislation required the reporting of abuse and neglect. As priorities changed to placement prevention in the late seventies and early eighties, the foster care population showed a decrease for 5 straight years. The population of at-risk children (0-18 years of age) has increased statewide from 2,414,000 in fiscal year 1982-1983 to the current figure (fiscal year 1990-1991) of 3,058,988 and has resulted in the increase of the foster care population every year since 1983.

Innovation in Service Delivery:
The Intensive Crisis Counseling Program

Florida's recognition of its pattern of growth in the foster care population plus the increasing number of children reported for abuse

Table 5.1   The Growth in the Average Daily Foster Care Population and Reports of Child Abuse and Neglect During Selected Years Between 1970 and 1991

FY	Average Daily Population in FC	Number of Children Reported	Number of Reports
1970-1971	unavailable	4,225	unavailable
1971-1972	4,459	13,983	unavailable
1972-1973	4,918	25,853	unavailable
1975-1976	6,319	38,704	unavailable
1978-1979	8,118	60,840	30,892
1980-1981	7,190	68,900	41,495
1982-1983	6,090	65,870	45,704
1984-1985	6,507	84,923	57,704
1986-1987	6,755	unavailable	84,849
1988-1989	7,605	138,703	106,974
1989-1990	8,139	182,291	119,374

and neglect and the increasing number of abuse and neglect reports brought about a refocusing of prevention and treatment efforts.

In 1980 the legislature, through the efforts of people like Senator Jack Gordon of Miami, provided $200,000 to fund two pilot, home-based programs to try to slow this growth. A rural area, Panama City, and an urban area, Miami, were chosen as sites to test the concept of providing in-home services to families who were in crisis and in danger of having their children removed from the home. The Homebuilders model, in use in Tacoma, Washington, was already showing signs of successful intervention with these types of families. The Homebuilders claimed a success rate of up to 97%. Florida adopted this model for implementation as its own preventive placement services model.

In 1981, $200,00 divided equally between the two contracted pilots, purchased 2½ full-time equivalent (FTE) positions in each pilot to work intensively with the families. Small caseloads of four families per FTE and staff availability to the family 24 hours a day were seen as key elements in the initial and subsequent success of the program. These pilots, which we called Intensive Crisis Counseling Programs (ICCP), began to work with families in February 1981. Provider staff were trained in the Homebuilders method prior to beginning their work with these families. Although the Homebuilders model was used to train our contract providers, ICCP differed from their model in several ways.

Caseloads in ICCP were larger, with each FTE expected to serve 32 families per year compared to 20 in Homebuilders. Referrals came from protective investigators (intake) and child protective supervision counselors while Homebuilders took their referrals from any community agency and from self-referrals. Psychotic and severely emotionally disturbed clients who might be seen by other Homebuilders projects were not seen in the Florida Intensive Crisis Counseling programs.

Evaluation of ICCP

The first departmental evaluation of the ICCP program occurred 20 months after program start-up. Success rates at case closure were high (86%), with subsequent success rates at 1 month of 85.7%, at 3 months of 65.5%, and at 6 months of 80.0%.[2] Shelter placements showed an adjusted decrease of 20.25% between the two pilots after factoring in the overall statewide decrease in the shelter population. Dispositions to foster care also showed an adjusted decrease of 20% after the first 20 months of ICCP services. Although a causal relationship between this new home-based service and a reduction in shelter and foster care could not be determined, families were being taught new skills and new methods to deal with crises, and most of these children were not coming into the state's care.

With the success of the ICCP program came a vote of confidence from the legislature and departmental administrators that a truly effective family preservation service was having an impact on the system and the families it served. This confidence continued and within 5 years funding had grown from $200,000 in 1981 to $1.5 million in fiscal year 1986-1987 when the program finally became available in all 11 districts within the state's Department of Health and Rehabilitative Services (HRS). By 1989, ICCPs were available in all 67 counties in the state.

The success of the ICCP model has been attributed to several things. Its availability in all 67 counties assures that all HRS child welfare units have access to the service, although rather limited in some areas of the state. Response time to referrals is within 24 hours. Many of the contracted providers require master of social work degrees even though HRS requires only a bachelor's degree and 2 years' experience in a social work or counseling position.

The ICCP model combines both concrete and psychological services (the securing of resources and providing of therapy) in a mix that will stabilize a family in crisis, provide for their immediate needs by identifying and setting up needed services, and teach families how to handle similar crises when they occur. All this occurs within a 6-week time span at a current cost of $1,590 per family served (1990-1991 fiscal year estimate).

Success rates have remained stable at case closure and have actually shown improvement at 6- and 12-month intervals, as depicted in Table 5.2. *Success* as we define it means that the family, including the target child, were intact during the time period covered. Target children who were placed out of the home by the agency or family or who were runaways during the review period were considered unsuccessful regardless of the period of time they were gone. Our stricter definition of success has actually resulted in a lower success rate than might be expected because some of these target children were reported as absent from the home because parents were in residential treatment. Some may have voluntarily placed their children temporarily with other family members due to financial or emotional stress (a legitimate response to stress families may have learned from their ICCP counselor), but were counted as unsuccessful for that time period.

Follow-up with some families was often difficult due to the families' mobility. Therefore, follow-up data were only gathered on those families that could be located, or that had an open case with the department.

In July 1991, the department's ability to collect follow-up data on families changed when ICCP became a part of the department's client information systems data base. Since that date, all clients are registered by the provider in the client data base for purposes of tracking their progress. Reasons for terminating cases have expanded because of access to this data base, resulting in an accurate picture of why clients are terminated from ICCP. Follow-up is easier because this data base is statewide and provides more information on clients if they are referred again to the department for any subsequent reasons including delinquency, dependency, or status referrals. If the client was placed in care such as shelter, detention, foster care, or a delinquency program, we are able to calculate how many days were spent in that program as well as the type of placement and the reason for placement.

As funding for ICCP has increased each year since its inception in 1981 to a current budget of $4,788,000 in fiscal year 1991-1992, the demand for program availability has also increased. Some providers report being able to respond to only 50% of the need in their geographic area. Families appear to be in need of longer term in-home services due

Table 5.2   ICCP Success Rates (in percentages)

FY	Case Closure	0-6 Months	6-12 Months
1986-1987	87.3	—	61.8
1987-1988	78.4	71.0	71.5
1988-1989	82.5	78.0	79.4
1989-1990	80.7	78.0	79.8

to the severity of stressors such as lost or unstable employment, drug and alcohol abuse, and a reduction in available community resources. ICCP providers began to take second referrals on families, though they were initially reluctant to do so. The average length of service in number of days provided to families began to increase and the overall success rate at case closure began to decrease. As a result, the Department of Health and Rehabilitative Services began to look at other models and additional funding sources for answers to these problems.

Improving Services for Families and Children At Risk: The Intensive Family Service Model (IFS)

Representative Elaine Bloom of Miami expressed a strong interest in what other states were doing in family preservation services. The models in use in other states such as New York, Connecticut, New Jersey, and Maryland were reviewed. A model similar to the state of Maryland's model of Intensive Family Services (IFS) was adopted by Florida in response to and in addition to the ICCP funded programs.

Although ICCP had begun to expand the type of clients eligible for ICCP services to include delinquents, mental health, foster care, and adoption disruptions as early as 1988-1989, the IFS program could only focus on dependent clients because initial funds were severely limited. Clients who were referred to the department for abuse or neglect, and who were in danger of removal from their home within 30 days if services were not put in place, were eligible for these new IFS services.

IFS was a response to the ICCP program's need to work for a longer period of time (3 months) with some families who, though not in imminent danger of removal, were likely to be removed within one month if needed services were not provided. Because so many of the families had multiple needs, a 6-week intervention program did not appear to offer enough, especially considering the lack of other adequately funded resources. IFS was seen as a possible answer.

A 15-month pilot program was created in Ocala and Sarasota using existing ICCP funds. The contract providers in each city were awarded $70,000 to work with families. The IFS model differed from ICCP in that it provided up to 3 months of in-home services, had a budget of $500 per family of flexible dollars to purchase essential goods and services for the family, had funding to purchase psychological and psychiatric services including testing, evaluations, and staff case consultation, and employed the use of a paraprofessional aide. This paraprofessional aide was used to transport family members to needed services; teach new skills such as parenting and communication to family members; and locate, arrange, and ensure that other needed services were provided to the family. As a team member, the paraprofessional aide's role was seen as critical to the success of the program. Caseload sizes were small (6 families per counselor and paraprofessional aide) when compared to protective services caseloads that sometimes exceeded 35 to 1, but were larger than ICCP's 4 to 1 ratio and some Homebuilders models that were as low as 2 families to 1 caseworker. Sarasota and Ocala, although not considered large communities, had at-risk populations in excess of 45,000 children. Some community resources are available to provide other follow-up services to these families.

The original project design involved comparison of data between IFS and ICCP families served, with a hypothesis that IFS families, because they had longer treatment periods, flexible funds, readily available psychological and psychiatric services, and a paraprofessional aide to complement the caseworker, would demonstrate a higher rate of success.

Evaluating IFS

In order to test this hypothesis, we attempted to match an equal number of ICCP and IFS families, based on characteristics including reason for referral to the department, age of the target child, prior history of allegations, response to treatment efforts, overall risk level, and marital status of the natural parents. Matching of the families was the responsibility of the ICCP and IFS providers in each pilot city and this match was to occur during the initiation of services. Data were collected that included pre- and posttesting of the levels of family functioning, demographic information, types and intensities of outside services provided, tracking of the use of flexible dollars (IFS clients only), and calculation of the type and amounts of casework services provided by the aide and caseworker.

While data were available on all families for each of the above characteristics, none of the families could be matched using all of the characteristics and most families could only be matched on a few of the items. In addition, the sample sizes in both IFS and ICCP were too small to provide meaningful and reliable data. This forced us to abandon our hypothesis for the two groups after about 10 months of collecting comparison data. Data collection for IFS families, however, continued through June 1991 and the department is now preparing its final report on the success of the pilots.

The analysis of the first 10 months of data collected suggests that IFS was successful with 83% of the families served at case closure, 90% successful 2 months following case closing, and 81% and 80% successful at 4 and 6 months, respectively, following case closure. Success is defined as "no children were removed from the home due to subsequent abuse or neglect and placed into substitute care including shelter, foster care or with other relatives."

Pre- and posttesting of family functioning was completed with all IFS families served, using portions of the "Children and Family Services Intake Assessment" tool that has been used by Maryland's IFS program. Items measured included: Prior agency history, employment status, residential stability, home condition, supervision in the home, caretaker supports, caretaker cooperation, emotional stability of the primary caretaker, and caretaker substance abuse. Items specific to the child at highest risk included self-care ability, fear factors, perpetrator access, and the child's behavior. Each item was scored jointly by the caseworker and aide within the first week of service based on their own observations and available data, and then again at case closure (whether the case outcome was successful or not).

Comparison of test results show that "caretaker cooperation" was the one area most likely to be rated at high risk. We hypothesize that the reason this factor was the highest risk indicator measured was that many families who entered into treatment did so with an apparent hostile or apprehensive attitude toward the agency or caseworker because of the ever-present threat of and the agency's legal authority to remove the children from the home if necessary. By the time IFS began working with the family the police, protective investigators, the child protection team, and others had become intimately involved in the investigation of abuse/neglect.

In contrast, "caretaker cooperation" was also one of the areas where the most improvement occurred. We believe the reason for such an improvement in this area was a family's increased comfort level when dealing with the IFS caseworker and their realization that IFS was there to truly help the family by providing services and keeping the children in the home. Nearly all 29 families taking part in the testing showed much improvement as measured through pre- and posttesting. Few families got worse in any category. Home conditions improved in slightly less than half the families served.

Preliminary data on IFS shows the program to be at least as successful as ICCP at case closure. The first follow-up at 2 months shows a higher success rate in IFS with comparable success rates at the 4- to 6-month follow-ups when compared to ICCP. Because the client data base was so small, no attempt was made to compare the success rates of specific types of referrals, such as sexual abuse, with other types of referrals.

The probability of success of IFS families appears to depend on several factors. Some of these factors include the availability and accessibility of community resources; the inclusion of both concrete and clinical services in the case plan; low worker caseloads; the availability of flexible dollars; parental commitment to keeping the child in the home; timely response to a crisis; the emotional stability of the family members; and the understanding and commitment to make it work on the part of the referring agency, courts, and others involved.

Financial instability was a common factor in most IFS cases. An average of $436 in flexible funds per family were spent, usually for child care (while waiting for at-risk subsidized child-care slots to open up, or for after school care) clothing, rent payments/deposits, utility payments, transportation, and vehicle assistance.

Total program costs and costs per family served are not yet calculated. However, at an estimated cost of $3,000 per family served, if just one child per family is prevented from going into out-of-home care, the cost avoidance to the agency per year in just the foster care board rate alone is one and one-half times the cost of providing IFS services to an entire family. If medical care, clothing allowances, and agency staff costs are factored in, then the cost avoidance grows.

In-home family preservation programs that utilize the team model, as IFS does, appear to be successful, not only in Florida but also in other states. Success rates of 80% and higher were common for both IFS pilots. Evaluation measures show improvements in family functioning. Caseworker and paraprofessional aides as a team are able to offer more services to families than the traditional single caseworker can. Sexual abuse cases and cases of drug-involved caretakers have been served successfully—at least from the initial IFS data collected—provided some safety measures are put in place for the child and the perpetrator is involved in specialized interventions in combination with IFS. Families can be taught how to respond appropriately to the crisis of alleged and/or confirmed sexual abuse.

Standardization of Family Preservation Services on a Statewide Basis

In 1990, while the IFS program was gearing up, legislation was introduced that formally set up standards for family preservation programs in Florida. Representative Elaine Bloom of Miami proposed legislation that called for the establishment of the Family Builders programs. Although the legislation provided no separate budget for the creation of the programs, standards were set for who would be served. Program goals were established, caseload sizes were established, and staff qualifications were clearly defined. With this legislation enacted, Florida may be one of only a few states with statewide standards for family preservation programs.

Family Builders Program

During the 1991 legislative session, revisions to the Family Builders statute were enacted and $3.2 million dollars was appropriated to implement a Family Builders model in four HRS districts (Jacksonville, Tampa, Orlando, and Miami).

During fiscal year 1990-1991 the average length of stay in emergency shelter care rose to 33.5 days, followed by an average length of stay in foster care of up to 26.2 months. Once children were removed from the home the likelihood that they would experience three or more placements due to an overcrowded substitute care system increased. All too frequently, court involvement inhibited voluntary participation by the family in resolving problems within the family unit. Because of crowded court dockets and multiple judicial continuances, court reviews for children in substitute care placement would be postponed and the rights of children to permanent homes were severely compromised. It was clear that not only must there be an immediate response capability to prevent placement but enhanced reunification efforts were also necessary to return children home from substitute care and, in some cases, to prevent adoption disruptions. The Florida Family Builders model program was crafted to meet several goals:

- Assure the safety of children in their own homes
- Preserve intact families
- Impact, positively, the rising incidence of emergency shelter and foster care placements
- Enhance reunification efforts to return children home from foster care
- Prevent adoption disruptions
- Demonstrate the cost avoidance of providing preventive services over out-of-home placement

The target populations to be served include children at immediate risk of removal from the home while a child abuse investigation is being completed; families under protective supervision where removal of the child is imminent; children in subsidized adoption placements in jeopardy of disruption; and children in foster care for less than 30 days who have the goal of reunification, but where intensive efforts are required to stabilize the family and prepare them for the safe return of the child.

On October 1, 1991, four Family Builders programs were implemented through a purchase of service mechanism in Jacksonville, Tampa, Orlando, and Miami. Each program is composed of three Family Builders units. A unit includes one coordinator, two treatment teams (one counselor and one paraprofessional aide per team), and one clerical staff person. The maximum caseload per treatment team does not exceed six families and the service period is up to 3 months per family.

In order to become a selected provider of Family Builders services, the agency must have demonstrated expertise in the delivery of family preservation services and in the utilization of other community support groups and resources. Prior to accepting families referred for service by HRS, the Family Builders professional staff must complete 80 hours of preservice training as prescribed by HRS. Within the first 90 days of operation the paraprofessional staff and supervisory staff must have completed 27 hours of training.

Program Features

In addition to small caseloads these treatment teams have access to flexible funds (averaging $500 per family) to acquire items such as food, clothing, transportation, rent deposits, utility payments, and so on, when the family is not eligible to receive these items from any other source. Additional funds are provided to pay for evaluation and diagnostic services for the families as well as supplemental expert consultation services for the Family Builders staff in working with high-risk families. These Family Builders programs will serve the families at highest risk, such as drug-involved and sexual abuse cases.

By the close of the first 9 months of operation, it is anticipated that 430 families will have been served, that 87% of the children served will have avoided a substitute care placement or have been reunified with their families as a result of a shortened length of stay, and that the cost avoidance in emergency shelter and foster care will reach approximately $3.8 million by fiscal year 1992-1993.

Evaluation of the Family Builders Programs

As the Family Builders programs begin operation, the Department of Health and Rehabilitative Services is preparing to enter into a contract with Florida State University, School of Social Work, to evaluate the quality of these programs, determine their effectiveness, and the overall cost avoidance of family preservation services. The total budget for the evaluation is $150,000 and will extend over a period of 13 months.

As a part of the evaluation the university will identify or develop and recommend to the department several instruments that will provide demographic and psychosocial characteristics of the families served, program and client outcome data, family functioning levels based upon both pre- and posttesting, and agency and client satisfaction surveys. The impact of the services will be evaluated at the time of case closure and at 3- and 6-month intervals thereafter. The effect of flexible dollars upon client success rate will be measured as well as a measure of social and environmental characteristics of the families prior to and following intervention. The evaluation project will also include a comparison group of families who, although eligible for Family Builders services, were not served because of full caseloads. These families will be included in the 3- and 6-month follow-up.

This particular evaluation is unique in that it begins during the formative period of the Family Builders program and is designed so that, should second-year funding for the evaluation not be provided, the Department would be able to continue the evaluation design through to completion. It is also unique in that it provides for the comparison study of families served and families, though eligible for services, that were not served due to full caseloads. The first year's report will be completed in late 1992.

Summary

As so many other states are learning, there is no "one size fits all" program response to family preservation. We need to continue the resources and programs that allow for an immediate crisis response and also provide for the longer term, intensive in-home services program that will build upon the strengths of families and empower them to raise their children adequately in a safe environment. There will continue to be a need for the substitute care system but, through the provision of multiple family preservation services and programs, it is expected that more children can be maintained safely in their own homes. Reunification of those children who must be removed from their homes can be expedited and a positive impact can be made in those homes where an adoptive placement may disrupt causing yet another child to lose the benefit of a permanent family.

Florida's 10 years of experience in family preservation services, its high success rate in keeping families intact and safe, and its flexibility and willingness to be creative in its program design to meet the needs of the families it serves, continue to be the elements of a highly successful alternative to substitute care. Continued legislative and community support of these programs will help keep Florida at the forefront of family preservation while at the same time teach families how to safely respond to crisis.

Notes

1. This was confirmed in a survey of all 50 states by the National Committee for Prevention of Child Abuse in the fall of 1982. There were cutbacks in staff or service dollars in 32 states and only 5 states reported no increase in child abuse and neglect.

2. The decrease in effectiveness at 3 months was due to logistics involved in initial data collection efforts and not attributable to any other reason.

6

The Relative Effectiveness of Family Preservation Services With Neglectful Families

MARIANNE BERRY

With increases in reports of child abuse and concomitant reductions in federal funding, child welfare services are becoming increasingly focused on child protection, to the detriment of more general services to promote the child's welfare. State agencies, by necessity, are forced by public pressure and funding constraints to provide for the reporting and investigation of child abuse, while other services to improve family functioning of non-crisis-level families are neglected (Kamerman & Kahn, 1989). Family preservation programs are targeted at such families in crisis, with the belief that families in crisis are more amenable to assistance and change (Barth, 1990). This chapter describes an intensive family preservation program that uses an ecological and case management model of treatment, presents findings from an evaluation

AUTHOR'S NOTE: Support for this research was provided by the American Association of University Women. The author thanks Jo Ann Cook and Mark Claycomb at Children's Home Society of California and Rick Barth at the University of California School of Social Welfare for assistance with this study, and Mark Fraser at the University of Utah and Kevin Grigsby at the University of Georgia for comments on earlier versions of the chapter.

Some of the evaluation results reported in this chapter were also reported in an article by the author published as "An Evaluation of Family Preservation Services: Fitting Agency Services to Family Needs," *Social Work* (1992).

of the program, and poses resultant questions about the role of family preservation services in the larger sphere of child welfare services.

Case management and service coordination are two related methods child welfare agencies are using to help provide services to families, and these methods are not only useful for the child protective services caseworker, they also contribute to the efficacy of home-based placement prevention efforts. In family preservation programs, case management and service coordination are important components of an ecological approach with an emphasis on client empowerment (Allen, 1990). One of the basic tenets of family-centered practice and short-term treatment is that, for services to be effective and for progress to continue after services have concluded, resources and supports in the family's social environment must be mobilized and strengthened (Lovell & Hawkins, 1988; Polansky & Gaudin, 1983; Stehno, 1986). Families who are isolated with few social supports are at greater risk of child abuse and neglect (Cochran & Brassard, 1979; Saulnier & Rowland, 1985), and are less likely to have their children returned if placed into foster care (Maluccio & Whittaker, 1988). Thus formal and informal social resources have become an important component of permanency planning practice and family preservation services, and the effective case manager helps to assess the need for supports and to coordinate the acquisition of these supports for the family.

Family preservation programs are based on the proposition that this type of placement prevention services includes whatever it takes to improve family relations and keep the family together. This commitment requires round-the-clock availability of workers, a wide range of skills and resources, and the ability to work within the family's ecological system, including the community. Thus the family preservationist seeks to mobilize the family in crisis to learn new skills and acquire needed resources through on-site, hands-on assessment, counseling, and teaching.

The Environment of Families At Risk

Families who abuse or neglect their children are often termed multi-problem families or families out of control (Garbarino, 1977). Instead of being viewed as a problem associated with the psychopathology of parents (Spinetta & Rigler, 1972), child abuse is part of a more general phenomenon of maltreatment of children (Garbarino, 1977; Gil, 1973), and, as such, should be addressed as a product of the interplay of individual behavior and the societal environment surrounding children and families (Friedman, 1976; Polansky, 1976).

Research in child abuse and neglect indicates that maltreating parents are likely to have few or impotent resources for coping (McClelland, 1973). They are isolated from social networks and other sources of modeling and support (Polansky & Gaudin, 1983). They have histories of deprivation, mental illness, and low self-esteem (Gaines, Sandgrund, Green, & Power, 1978; Garbarino, 1976; Paulson, Afifi, Chaleff, Liu, & Thomason, 1975; Shapiro, 1980), and are often, but not always, from a lower socioeconomic group (Garbarino, 1976; Shapiro, 1980). These resource deficits and stressors contribute to family tension and a way of life that promotes antisocial and aggressive behavior. In addition to these resource deficits, individuals in abusive families also have fewer than average positive exchanges within the family to reinforce prosocial behavior, and greater than average negative and coercive exchanges (Patterson, 1982). These patterns over time provide a stressful and demanding family environment, and decrease the number of reinforcers and resources for individuals, especially mothers (Patterson, 1980).

Wahler and Dumas (1984) have identified abuse to occur in families with insular mothers. *Insularity* is defined as "a specific pattern of social contacts within the community that are characterized by a high level of negatively perceived coercive interchanges with relatives and/or helping agency representatives and by a low level of positively perceived supportive interchanges with friends" (Wahler & Dumas, 1984, p. 387). Those children with insular mothers are at risk of abuse because these mothers have limited opportunities to diffuse stress and also have few models of positive interaction. Increasing and developing supportive networks for these mothers can help to diffuse the stress and help mothers in managing day-to-day stress without abusing their children.

Crises like child abuse occur when stressors outweigh resources. Stressors correlated with child abuse include "different" child characteristics (such as prematurity or mental retardation), marital difficulties, unemployment, unwanted pregnancy, and crowded living conditions (Parke & Collmer, 1975). These stressors, if not adequately resolved or managed, can pile up over time to produce great social stress, often a precursor of abuse. "It is the unmanageability of the stress which is the most important factor and unmanageability is a product of a mismatch between the level of stress and the availability and potency of support systems" (Garbarino, 1977, p. 727).

Changes in economic and family structure in the recent past amplify the importance of support for families. The increase in the mobility of the American family has resulted in a decline in support from extended family. Many families no longer live in the same neighborhood or city with other relatives, reducing availability of baby-sitting and child care, as well as social and recreational opportunities.

In exploring the ecological paradigm in child, youth, and family services, Whittaker, Schinke, and Gilchrist (1986) propose the two essential elements of an ecologically oriented intervention: "building more supportive, nurturant environments for clients through various forms of environmental helping that are designed to increase social support, and improving clients' competence in dealing with both prox- imate and distal environments through the teaching of specific life skills" (p. 492). These two elements are crucial to the development of resources for impoverished families, families who may lack monetary, informational, and social and/or emotional resources.

The ecological approach to child abuse and neglect thus looks beyond personal and "intrapsychic" determinants of abuse, and recognizes the effect the environment, both within the family and within the larger political, economic, and social spheres, has on behavior. "It directs our attention to personally impoverished families clustered in socially im- poverished places: high-risk families in high-risk neighborhoods" (Garbarino, 1981, p. 237).

Since many insular mothers may indeed be stressed more than helped by interchanges with relatives and friends (Tracy, 1990; Van Meter, Haynes, & Kropp, 1987; Wahler & Dumas, 1984), social support in a more formal (than informal) sense may be needed by multistressed families. Sustaining informal networks may be more stressful than productive to isolated parents (Belle, 1982; Tracy, 1990), and linking families with more formal services and supports, if sensitive and mean- ingful, may be appropriate. Formal services do not necessarily entail involving a family in a long-term and complicated system of intrusive family services, such as child protective services. Formal social support can be any agency that offers help to families, such as the housing bureau, food stamps, day-care centers and schools, and hospitals. Through ecologically oriented family preservation services, families can be helped to negotiate the maze of applying for the supportive services these agencies offer, and need not be permanently enrolled in any particular course of action provided by these agencies. Often, simply making families aware of these resources for their future use is enough. Other families may need to be guided through initial utilization of services in order to ensure that the family understands and can repeat the process.

An equally important form of social support identified by Whittaker and colleagues (1986) is the teaching of specific life skills. This more tangible and concrete form of social support is especially applicable in short-term interventions where the less tangible emotional support from agency workers is available for a finite period, usually 2 to 3 months. The skill-building that occurs will continue to support and reinforce positive family interaction in the long run, after formal services have ended.

Intensive Family Preservation Programs as Resource Locators and Builders

When child abuse and neglect are defined as a result of social isolation and overwhelming stress, then the solution is identified as eliminating or reducing that isolation and stress. Intensive family preservation services are aimed at linking families with resources in their family and community that they have not utilized, and of which they may not be aware. The resources that these programs provide include money, help with housing and food, education about child rearing and job skills, modeling of housecleaning and shopping skills, transportation, and improvement of family communication patterns. As previously enumerated, these resources run the gamut from the basics such as food and shelter to more intangible and elusive resources such as fostering love and affection between family members.

Family preservation programs are viewed as a mediating influence between family stress and family breakdown (as evidenced by child placement). Ecological family preservation programs assess family stressors and resources and help to bolster and increase the family's resources to the point that the stressors that are associated with risk of placement can be ameliorated. The In-Home Family Care program offered by the Children's Home Society of California is one such ecologically oriented program, and has conducted ongoing evaluations to assess the effectiveness of services based on this model.

The In-Home Family Care Program

The In-Home Family Care program began in 1980 in San Francisco as the Emergency Family Care Program of San Francisco Home Health

Service as a 3-year demonstration project. It has always been based on a case management model, emphasizing time-limited, task-centered treatment that is systems-based and environmentally oriented (Remy & Hanson, 1982). Installing this type of program within the Home Health Service was intended to reduce the political and "turf" disputes in San Francisco concerning which child welfare agencies should sponsor an emergency program, but this choice of auspices affected the reputation of the program, both positively and negatively (Remy & Hanson, 1982).

The program was immediately embraced by the child welfare community. Referrals have always exceeded program acceptance rates. Given that the program was associated with a home health agency, however, early evaluations showed that many referring community agencies viewed the program merely as a health-homemaker service, and thus referred low-risk, well-functioning families, instead of families at true risk of child placement (Remy & Hanson, 1982). About one third of referrals in the early 1980s were from hospitals, reflecting this health-homemaker orientation. Another third of program referrals came from the public child protective services agency, but most of these were from the ongoing service units, rather than the Emergency Services Unit, reflecting a majority of chronic problem cases rather than true emergency and imminent risk cases.

At the end of the 3-year demonstration period, the program was transferred to Children's Home Society of California for inclusion in their varied range of services (Remy & Hanson, 1983). The name of the program was changed in 1989 from Emergency Family Care to In-Home Family Care, to emphasize the home-based focus of treatment. In 1991, the In-Home Family Care program was discontinued in the Oakland office of Children's Home Society of California due to funding constraints, but continues to grow in San Francisco and Los Angeles.

The Treatment Model

The In-Home Family Care program offers intensive family preservation services within an ecological framework. The program is one of the many services provided by Children's Home Society of California. The program emphasizes strengthening the family's social and ecological system, and does not follow a conventional family therapy model. Family care workers do whatever it takes to help the family acquire tangible resources, including finding housing and day care for the family, if necessary.

The primary goal of services is to prevent the need for out-of-home placement. This usually entails resolving immediate crises and teaching skills necessary for the independent maintenance of family integrity. This requires some level of proficiency at problem solving and communication skills, but therapists also provide such concrete services as housecleaning and transportation. By so doing, a worker models how to do these skills, and also demonstrates his or her commitment to the family (Kinney, Haapala, Booth, & Leavitt, 1988). During the provision of such "hard" services, therapists can also observe clients' skills and talk about other problems the family is experiencing. In this way, the round-the-clock and across-the-board availability and participation of the therapist is truly a comprehensive family service.

The target population. The In-Home Family Care program emphasizes working with families at imminent risk of removal of the child. Degree of risk is determined by the Department of Social Services if that is the referral source. If the referral is from another source, the intake worker determines the degree of risk after discussion with the referral source and based on the prior placement history of the family as well as other risk factors.

Removal of a child and placement into foster care is intended to prevent continued harm to the child or the potential for danger to the child in the home. Parental and child factors associated with child abuse and neglect abound in the research literature, and these factors are included in the many risk assessment tools being developed and in use in many states (Johnson & L'Esperance, 1984; Magura & Moses, 1986; Pecora, 1988). Such factors include social isolation, a parent's history of being abused in childhood, social and economic stress, and substance abuse. An assessment of these factors within any one family can be a good predictive tool for risk of abuse.

While there are a variety of factors that may predict whether a child is in danger of abuse, however, there are additional factors that determine whether a child is removed from the home; some concerning the same intrafamilial characteristics and problems, and others concerning the availability of foster homes, reporting mechanisms, and so on. Thus there can be a wide disparity between the children identified as being at risk of abuse and those who would actually become placement statistics without intervention (AuClaire & Schwartz, 1986; Tracy, 1991; Yuan & Struckman-Johnson, 1991). The factors that predict placement are not always included in risk assessment tools, which may focus on parent-child interaction, and disregard other environmental factors or systemic decision-making factors. Many studies have shown that, despite the reluctance to place for reasons of poverty (Pelton, 1989), the income level of the family is often a key predictor of whether a child is removed, over and above the severity of abuse or neglect (Katz, Hampton, Newberger, Bowles, & Snyder, 1986; Lindsey, 1991).

Many programs like Homebuilders agree that placement is imminent if the child's protective service worker details a plan to place the child within 24 to 48 hours (Kinney et al., 1988), but this places the assessment of risk in the hands of child protective service workers, who may judge imminence of placement in a variety of ways. Other family preservation programs broaden imminent risk to include families with many risk factors, such as prior placement, a history of abuse, or a out-of-control adolescent (Pecora, Fraser, Haapala, & Bartlomé, 1987; Showell, Hartley, & Allen, 1987). These programs may limit their population to child protective service cases, or they can use these risk factors to define other families as soon-to-be child protective service cases, and thus, another entré to a designation of imminent risk of placement. Therefore, determination of risk level can vary greatly from program to program and needs to follow very specific and reliable guidelines (Tracy, 1991).

The In-Home Family Care program first defined families at risk (in 1983) as those families in which the following were true:

1. the referral came from the Department of Social Services,
2. the family had more than one child, and
3. the family was of minority ethnicity (Remy & Hanson, 1983).

Since 1983, risk has been further specified as pertaining to families with any of the following characteristics:

1. a child currently in placement,
2. a child with a prior history of placement,
3. a family history of abuse or neglect,

or if more than one of the following are true:

1. multiproblem family,
2. a multiracial family,
3. possible abuse,

4. an absent parent,
5. parental substance abuse, psychiatric history, developmental disability, or severe physical illness.

Once families are deemed to be at risk of child placement, each child in the family is also assessed as to his or her degree of imminence of risk of placement: within 72 hours, within 2 months, or more than 2 months away. Few programs in the literature specify such a categorization of imminence of risk (Tracy, 1991). Some families may be deemed to be at imminent risk, but may have only one child out of five at imminent (within 72 hours) risk of placement, and the other children might be at lesser risk levels. Unfortunately, the program does not keep standard information on the nature of the crisis event that precipitates referral for a given family; such information would be very useful in an examination of the target population.

In this program, families may be deemed ineligible if there is too much danger to the worker, other help is available, no children are at risk, parents are unavailable, parents decline service, or all children are older than 14 years of age. Families are not excluded due to mental retardation or substance abuse, as they are in other family preservation programs (AuClaire & Schwartz, 1986; Landsman, 1985). Referrals to the program come from a variety of sources, including hospitals, the Department of Social Services, private social services, public health agencies, and self-referrals.

Program goals. The primary goal of intensive family preservation services is to prevent unnecessary out-of-home placement. A variety of intensive family preservation programs have been evaluated, and most report their placement prevention rate as the primary criterion of success. These programs report success rates ranging from 71% (Pecora et al., 1987) to 93% (Reid, Kagan, & Schlosberg, 1988), with Homebuilders averaging 90% of families intact at the end of treatment (Kinney et al., 1988). At the 1-year follow-up point, Homebuilders reports that 88% of families are still intact (Behavioral Sciences Institute, 1987), and Oregon's Intensive Family Services finds a 73% success rate (Showell, 1985). Most of these evaluations have been focused on imminent risk cases, but the determination of imminence is, again, diverse.

These services are meant to reduce a variety of risks, with prevention of placement being the primary goal. Of course, provision of these services should also reduce the risk of poor developmental outcomes for the child and continued abuse or neglect. Only a few evaluations of

preservation programs have addressed effects on the reduction of maltreatment factors, such as child behavior problems or family functioning (Kinney et al., 1988; Pecora et al., 1987). In the evaluation by
Nelson and colleagues (Nelson, 1991) of 11 family-based placement
prevention programs in six states, family preservation was associated
with the following changes during services: improvements in behavior,
material resources, family structure, family dynamics, emotional climate, perceptions of problems, community perceptions of the family,
informal support network, and community involvement. Those families
who had children removed had made significant declines in behavior,
family dynamics, emotional climate, community perception of the family, and community involvement. Given the short-term nature of these
preventive programs, this study does not answer the question of the
longevity of families' gains, particularly since the greatest gains were
made in the more intangible and elusive skills.

One evaluation of the Homebuilders program (Kinney et al., 1988)
reports that the majority of families improved in the child's school
attendance, hyperactivity, delinquent acts, and peer problems as judged
by the parent or a therapist at the end of treatment. However, all families
were judged to have remained the same regarding handling of medical
problems or physical handicaps, and the majority of families had remained the same regarding alcohol abuse or learning disabilities. Another
evaluation of the Homebuilders program looked at school adjustment,
delinquent behavior, home-related behavior, and cooperation with the
agency (Pecora et al., 1987). Except for cooperation, children in the
program made significant positive improvements during service. Parents also made significant improvements in supervision of younger
children, parenting of older children, attitudes toward preventing placement, and their knowledge of child care. In the Utah Family Preservation program (Pecora et al., 1987), children made significant gains in
school adjustment and behavior, and parents improved in parenting
behavior, attitudes, and knowledge.

The In-Home Family Care program seeks to improve the physical and
social family environment, with resulting impacts on child health,
behavior, safety, and development, and teaches family care skills to
parents with resulting impacts on parenting skills, environmental conditions, and acquisition of resources. Changes in these conditions and
skills are assessed through standardized instruments completed by the
family care worker at case opening, case closing, and at 1-month, 6-month,
and 1-year follow-up visits (copies of these forms are available from the

author). These assessment and tracking inventories were developed and evaluated during the pilot phase of the program (1980-1982), and have been completed on every case since 1983. The forms were modified in 1990 following the more recent program evaluation.[1]

Services provided. Following Whittaker and colleagues' (1986) framework, this program seeks both to increase social support and teach specific life skills. Depending on the family's presenting problems, workers may help parents to learn positive child-rearing skills instead of punitive and abusive patterns. They may also help families to acquire adequate housing and to apply for appropriate financial aid, as well as to learn how to budget the income they do have. Family care workers address any problems in the condition of the family's building or living unit, and help parents to fix broken windows and plumbing as well as helping to convince landlords to fix the heat, which is often permanently on or permanently off. Families are taught health care and nutrition practices, and are directed to legal assistance, if needed. Families are thus assessed as to their resource deficits, and these deficits are replenished by skill building and resource mobilization, including support networks.

In-Home Family Care service is not a one-way street where workers only give resources that families are free to take. When a case is opened for intensive family preservation services, the worker and the family members make service agreements involving tasks that the worker and the family members agree to perform. Agreements are written and specify the task, who will perform it, and where, when and how often it will be performed. Objectives of service are to be specified in behavioral terms. For example, one such agreement may stipulate that the mother will make an appointment for her child to go to the pediatrician for a well-baby checkup. This would be followed by a task agreement that the mother would take the child to the appointment and that the worker would provide transportation. Everyone signs the agreement when it is acceptable, and workers track progress on tasks. New tasks are typically set at every meeting of family and worker.

Staff consists of master's level social workers and family care workers who usually have a bachelor's or master's degree. Each family is assigned a social worker and a family care worker. Cases are meant to be open for about 3 months. San Francisco workers carry two to five cases at a time, while Oakland workers carry three cases at a time. A team meeting is held weekly to allow the social worker and his or her family care workers to discuss all current cases and their status. The social worker and other family care workers offer treatment strategies and are good sources of information about community resources.

Summative Evaluation

The San Francisco and Oakland programs were recently evaluated to determine whether they were meeting their goals of preventing placement of families at risk. This evaluation examined the characteristics of families and services contributing to family preservation, including the match of services to resource deficits. Skill gains among the families in the program were evaluated as a measure of program success, in addition to placement prevention. More specific information on the study methodology is discussed elsewhere (Berry, 1992).

Placement Risk Among Families Served

The demographic characteristics of the families served were fairly homogeneous, and have been discussed in detail elsewhere (Berry, 1991). In sum, these were high-risk families: young, single-mother-headed families overburdened with many young children and few resources, such as food or a phone in the home, and an average monthly income of $572, including AFDC benefits.

The families served by this program had a variety of problems. More than half of all families were experiencing problems with economic and environmental conditions (67%) and/or family interaction problems (57%), which includes nonadjudicated abuse and neglect. Large numbers of families were beset by a parent's handicap or illness (30%), an emotionally disturbed parent (23%), a history of adjudicated child neglect (16%), an absent parent (14%), a child's handicap or illness (14%), child behavior problems (12%), and/or parental substance abuse (12%). Less common were the problems of parental pregnancy, emotional disturbance of child, adjudicated child abuse, child or parent developmental disability, deceased parent, and child delinquency.

The average level of family functioning at intake was poor, or 3.9 on a scale from 1 (very good) to 5 (very poor). Families who later suffered removals functioned at a somewhat lower level at intake (4.1) than those remaining intact (3.9). Families were remarkably cooperative with family care workers, averaging 1.5 on a scale from 1 (cooperative) to 5 (uncooperative). Interestingly, families who indicated that they had relatives "nearby, able to help" were more likely to have children placed following treatment. It is unknown how many of those children were placed with those relatives, so this evaluation is unable to say whether these relatives were a resource or a strain for families.

Determining imminence of risk of placement. Only 49 of the 367 families served (13%) were judged to be at imminent risk of child placement. There were differences between the two agencies in the latitude they had in serving families: about one third of the Oakland cases were imminent risk, while only 11% of the San Francisco cases were imminent risk. This is largely a result of the funding differences between the two counties; the Oakland office was constrained by county funding to serve imminent risk (or "reasonable efforts") cases, while the San Francisco office had more flexible funding definitions of their service population.

Imminent risk families were similar to general risk families, in that the majority had two or three children, almost three-quarters were headed by a single mother, the average age of the mothers was 31, an even number of children were male and female, and the average age of the children was 4.8 years. Imminent risk families were slightly, but not significantly, more likely to be African American. The majority of both imminent risk and general risk families had housing, food in the home, and a phone, and about three quarters in each group received AFDC and Medi-Cal. Imminent risk families were slightly less likely than general risk families to report that they had friends or relatives available to help them.

The imminent risk designation appears to be associated with standard risk factors. Imminent risk families were more likely to receive service primarily for substance abuse, parental handicap, or a request for child placement. Cases of a more general risk level were significantly more likely to receive service primarily for child emotional disturbance, child handicap, or economic/environmental conditions. There were no significant differences between imminent risk families and general risk families in the number of children in the home, ages of children in the home, mother's age, father's age, ethnicity, type of dwelling, or family income. The condition of the household at intake (crowded, disordered, dangerous, dirty, and/or uncomfortable) was significantly more of a serious problem for imminent risk families, as were child-care practices.

A discriminant analysis was performed to determine whether the key predictors identified by the program as imminent risk factors were used by the intake worker to define a family or a child to be at imminent risk of placement. The variables in the model included family characteristics (any prior removals, number of children, income, mother's age, and if any relatives were nearby), parents' presenting problems (abuse, neglect, developmental disability, and/or substance abuse), and parents' skills at intake (living conditions, discipline skills, and health care of children).

The key correlates of a determination of imminent risk of placement were prior removals, a low number of children in the family, parents' good health skills, and poor discipline skills at intake and poor living conditions. The presenting problem of abuse, neglect, developmentally disabled parent, or substance abuse were negligible in the designation of risk, as were the mother's age, the presence of relatives, or the income level of the family. This model was fairly poor at correctly classifying those children defined as imminent risk, with only 64% of cases correctly classified based on these factors. Therefore, intake workers were judging imminence of placement on factors besides those delineated by the program, or at random.

Mental capacity of families. Families suffering a child placement following services had been rated as more physically capable but less mentally capable of participating in service. A total of 38 families (10%) had a member with a developmental disability, either a parent (4%), a child (5%), or both (1%). When all indicators are collapsed to any developmental disability or mental incapacity in the family ($n = 50$), this is a significant contributor to child placement (a 24% placement rate vs. a 13% placement rate for all others; $\chi^2 = 3.71, p < .05$).

The presence of some mental incapacity appears to be a significant contributor to problems in the program. Mentally incapacitated families were somewhat more likely to have the problem of adjudicated child neglect, and significantly less likely to report the problems of child physical handicap or illness ($p < .05$) or economic or environmental conditions ($p < .01$). Mentally incapacitated families have a much higher placement rate, despite a greater likelihood of having the resources of food in the home and friends able to help them, and being no different from other families in the amount of time spent on a case, time spent in the home, and time spent in the agency. These families were judged by workers to be significantly less cooperative than mentally capable families. They were also more likely to have been referred by the Department of Social Services (20% vs. 11% of others were so referred, $\chi^2 = 4.46; p < .05$).

Service Components

Cases were served for an average of 77 days, or about 2½ months. The average family received 9.5 hours of service per week. Of course, the typical family received service intermittently, with some days of several hours of service and some days of little or no service. Families experiencing later removals were served an average of 12 days longer, an average of 148 minutes longer, and at an average of 45 minutes more per day, not significant differences.

Length of service varied with the presenting problems of the family (see Table 6.1). Cases for families who were treated for child neglect, child emotional disturbance, child abuse, or family interaction problems were open a significantly longer time than those for families without these problems. When the problems were those of an absent parent or a parent handicap or illness, service time was significantly shorter. The intensity of service also varied across presenting problems, with abusive families and those with child behavior problems receiving significantly less intensive service, averaging less than a hour of service per day. Those with the problems of an emotionally disturbed parent, an absent parent, or a handicapped parent received the most intensive service.

The proportion of time rather than the amount of time spent in the home was the relevant predictor of success. *No families experienced child placement when more than half of service time had been spent in the home.* Conversely, the placement rate skyrocketed to 28% (twice that of the entire sample) when more than half of service time had been spent in the agency. There were few differences in the proportions spent in the home or agency across different presenting problems.

Services provided. The most common service provided was that of case planning. This appears to be a catch-all category of service that does not provide much meaningful information about the type of service a family received (and the service log has since been revised by the agency to reflect more precisely those activities that were being coded as case planning). After case planning, families received large amounts of assessment, parent education, supplemental parenting, and teaching of family care. Families also received at least an hour of counseling, household maintenance, transportation, and referral services, on average.

The type of service provided made a difference in treatment success. Families that remained intact had received significantly larger amounts of time in supplemental parenting, teaching family care, and medical help. Families that experienced later placements had received some-

Table 6.1   Number of Days Open and Intensity of Service by
Presenting Problem

| Presenting Problem[a] | Mean No. of Days Case Open | | Intensity | Placement |
	W/Problem	W/O Problem	(hrs./week)	Rate (%)
Child neglect (n = 59)	104	72**	6.3	24
Child emotional disturbance (n = 28)	101	75*	6.8	18
Child abuse (n = 25)	101	75*	5.1	24
Parent developmental disability (n = 20)	96	76	9.2	25
Child behavior problem (n = 45)	93	75	5.5	18
Child developmental disability (n = 23)	87	76	7.8	22
Family interaction problems (n = 209)	87	64**	8.1	16
Economic/environmental (n = 243)	80	72	9.1	12
Parent emotional disturbance (n = 83)	79	76	11.2	10
Pregnancy (n = 32)	77	77	9.3	16
Parent substance abuse (n = 42)	71	78	7.7	19
Child handicap/illness (n = 52)	68	78	7.1	15
Parent absent (n = 50)	55	80**	16.7	10
Parent handicap/illness (n = 110)	49	89**	12.1	9

NOTE: a. Families can have up to four presenting problems.
* Difference is significant at .05 level.
** Difference is significant at .01 level.

what (but not significantly) larger amounts of assessment, crisis intervention, and help with housing and legal matters, and somewhat smaller
amounts of respite care, help in securing food, and parent education.

Family care workers utilize a variety of social supports in the provision of service to clients. Most of these collateral supports involve
formal agencies, particularly the Department of Social Services, and
private social service agencies. Other formal agencies commonly utilized in service are hospitals and public health agencies. Agencies with
specific contact with the children are an important collateral contact,
with 27% of cases involving respite care, 26% involving the schools,

and 21% involving nursery schools or day care. Friends (11%), relatives (10%), churches (10%), and talklines (23%) were the types of collateral contacts that involved more informal social support.

Whether or not a particular social resource was utilized did not make a difference in treatment outcome, but the amount of time spent with a collateral resource did make a difference: families remaining intact had workers who had spent somewhat more case time, on average, arranging help with talklines, private health care, day-care providers, and respite care.

Achievement of Program Goals

Placement prevention. The In-Home Family Care program is successful at preventing placement among the families it serves. Only 4% of families experienced placement while served by the program; another 6% experienced removals within 6 months after the case was closed, and a total of 12% of families had experienced placement by the 1-year follow-up point. This rate is comparable to rates reported for other family preservation programs in the nation.

Given that few families were judged to be at imminent risk of placement, such a high preservation rate is not surprising; what is surprising is that the placement rate for imminent risk families was no higher than that for families at a more general risk. A more detailed examination of the services provided and skills gained illuminates the services received by imminent risk families. Imminent risk cases received an average of 96 hours of service, or about 30 more hours, on average, than general risk cases. Of these 96 hours or so, an average of 40 hours were spent in the home, significantly more time than that for nonimminent cases (23 hours on average). Overall, the percentage of service time spent in the home versus that in the agency did not differ between imminent and general risk cases, but the intensity of service (average amount of time spent per day) was significantly different (4.5 hours vs. 1 hour per day). Imminent risk families received somewhat more time in case planning, supplemental parenting, crisis intervention, respite care, financial skills, and home health care, while general risk cases received more parent education, teaching of family care, and referrals to other services.[2]

Success rates are comparable when placements are counted by child, instead of by family. A total of 896 children were served in the 3-year period under study, and of those children, 96 or 11% were later placed in out-of-home care. The average length of time from case closing to child removal was 150 days, or about 5 months. Eight families experienced a child placement prior to the closing of the case, but services were continued to other children in the family.

Skill gains during treatment. The 327 families in the San Francisco program (data is not available on the Oakland program) made modest gains from the opening to the closing of a case, on average, and the largest numbers of families made gains in discipline, general child care, and encouragement of child development. Many families made no gains at all, however, especially in the areas of the crowdedness, orderliness, safety, cleanliness, and comfort of the household. More than a fifth of families actually declined from opening to closing in the areas of general child care, discipline, and encouragement of child development.

Families who remained together had begun service at significantly higher levels than placed families regarding the noncrowdedness, orderliness, cleanliness, and comfort of the home, the number of household resources and the physical condition of the household, and in health care and encouragement of child development (see Table 6.2). In addition, those families who remained intact had made significant improvements over the course of treatment (as judged by workers) in all areas, except for household safety, which remained relatively high across treatment. In comparison, those families who subsequently had a child removed had significantly deteriorated across treatment in the cleanliness of the home, and had deteriorated somewhat or had not improved in most other skills.

After a case was closed some of these gains deteriorated, as in the areas of safety and health care (judged at 1-month, 6-month, and 1-year follow-up visits). The areas that showed continued improvement, on average, were in general child-care skills, discipline and encouragement of child development, as well as orderliness and cleanliness of the household. Those families who made substantial gains from closing to the 6-month follow-up point in the areas of household cleanliness and the physical condition of the home were less likely to have children removed.

Given the association between specific skills and family preservation, the particular services provided may have an effect on program success. To test this hypothesis, the cases with data on the specific services provided were again examined in relation to their skill gains during care. The service of teaching family care was significantly associated with gains in the cleanliness, order, and comfort of the environment. Counseling was significantly associated with gains in

Table 6.2   Changes in Skills From Case Opening to Closing

Skill Area (total points)	Preserved		Placed	
	Opening (n = 207)	Closing (n = 207)	Opening (n = 34)	Closing (n = 34)
General Environment				
Noncrowdedness (5)	3.3	3.4*	3.2[a]	2.9
Orderliness (5)	3.6	3.7**	3.2[a]	3.2
Safety (5)	3.7	3.8	3.4	3.6
Cleanliness (5)	3.7	3.8*	3.6[a]	3.1*
Comfort (5)	3.5	3.6*	3.3[a]	3.2
Physical Environment				
Household resources (13)	9.8	10.3**	8.5[a]	8.7
Poor condition of building (13)	2.4	1.8**	2.5	2.7
Poor condition of living unit (18)	4.3	3.3**	5.8[a]	6.8
Child Care Skills				
General child care (42)	27.5	29.2**	25.0	25.1
Discipline (36)	21.4	22.9**	19.7	20.8
Health care/grooming (21)	13.4	14.3**	12.5[a]	12.1
Encourage development (33)	20.5	21.7**	18.8[a]	17.4

NOTE: a. Placed families were significantly poorer in skill area than preserved families at intake ($p < .05$).
* Change from case opening to closing (paired t test) is significant at .05 level.
** Change from case opening to closing (paired t test) is significant at .01 level.

cleanliness and health care skills. Help in securing food was significantly associated with gains in the cleanliness and order of the environment. Financial services were significantly associated with gains in the cleanliness, orderliness, and comfort of the environment. Provision of medical services, however, was significantly associated with a decline in the child-care skills of the parent. Perhaps the need for extensive medical services precluded the ability to make gains in child-care skills.

Skill gains were also examined in terms of their association with time spent in the home or the agency. Time at home visits and time in the agency were each associated with significant gains in the cleanliness of the environment, an increase in household resources, and an improvement in the physical condition of the living unit. The amount of time that a worker spent in the home was related to the environmental needs of the family, in that the amount of time in the home was greater where the intake levels of safety, cleanliness, and comfort of the home were worse. Workers spent more time in the homes that needed such improvements. Total case time as well as home time and agency time were also positively correlated with the poor physical condition of the building and the living unit at case opening. Workers spent more time both in the home and in the agency when the building and living unit were in worse physical shape. However, there was a positive correlation between the number of household resources a family had and the amount of time the worker spent. Workers spent more time (in total and in the agency) when it appeared as though there were resources there to utilize. These resources included separate bedrooms for parents and children, books, magazines, television, clock, and calendar.

There were no associations between the total time, time spent in the home, or the time spent in the agency with the client's initial levels of general child-care skills or specific skills regarding discipline, health care, or encouragement of development. Thus the initial assessment of the client's child-care skills did not affect how much time the worker eventually spent with that family, whereas more environmental aspects of the home were associated with worker time.

The Environment of Child Neglect

Given that child neglect was a presenting problem for 16% of the families served by this program, but was a problem among 27% of those experiencing child placement, *neglect was the most difficult presenting problem for this program to treat.* The environment of neglectful families has been well researched, and many of the demographic and environmental characteristics of neglectful families identified in other studies were corroborated in this sample (American Humane Association, 1988; Yuan & Struckman-Johnson, 1991). The families with an adjudicated child neglect problem prior to services were examined more closely, in order to identify possible reasons that services were not as effective for them. Such examination was possible in this analysis, given the sizeable proportion of families receiving services for child neglect.

Families referred by the Department of Social Services as neglectful families indeed displayed neglectful behavior. The neglect cases in this study were judged by workers to have significantly poorer family functioning than others, and to display poorer child-care skills, health care skills, and encouragement of child development. The level of household resources available to the family was rated much worse for neglect cases. More than a third of neglect cases had been referred by the Department of Social Services (compared to only 7% of other cases; $p < .001$). These cases were also much more likely to have had previous child removals (68% vs. 22%, $p < .001$).

The demographic characteristics of these families also substantiate findings from other neglect studies. The number of people in the household was significantly higher (4.1 vs. 3.7; $p < .05$). Neglectful families were slightly more likely to receive AFDC, but did not differ on any other household or social resources. Imminent risk of placement was judged by referring or intake workers to be significantly higher (4.4 vs. 3.5; $p < .05$), although the physical capability of the parent was judged to be better than average (4.6 vs. 3.9; $p < .001$). The proportion of neglect cases among blacks was especially high at 26%, compared to 17% for whites, 8% for Latinos, and 4% for Asians ($\chi^2 = 18.0$, $p < .05$). The problem of child neglect was not an isolated problem but was often associated with other presenting problems, especially child abuse, child developmental disability, child handicaps/illness, and parental substance abuse.

All of these stressors combine to result in an environment in great need of strengthening through the provision of resources and the building of family-care and home-care skills. Neglect is less the result of a crisis-producing incident than it is a chronic state of family disrepair. Neglectful families thus need service at least as intensive if not more intensive than that provided to most families, in order to mobilize needed resources and skills. This service should teach skills in the home and link families with more formal helping agencies in the neighborhood that can continue to help on a more long-term basis.

Services provided to neglectful families. The In-Home Family Care program was not very successful with neglect families, and an examination of the service provided to these families illustrates why. Neglect cases were open for a significantly longer time (104 days vs. 72 days), but received somewhat less service time overall (50 vs. 69 total hours of service). Therefore, the service provided to neglectful families was not as intensive as that provided to other families: neglect cases received an average of 6.3 hours of service per week, compared to 9.5 hours weekly for other families. While not a statistically significant difference, it is a provocative one.

There were no differences between neglect cases and others in the proportion of time spent in the home or agency. These families did receive significantly less time, however, at case planning, supplemental parenting, household maintenance, home health care, respite care, counseling, legal help, financial help, and help with housing ($p < .05$). Neglect cases were significantly less likely than other families to use private social services, public health agencies, mental health agencies, or schools as collateral contacts. Neglectful families were also significantly less skilled at closing in the areas of orderliness, safety, cleanliness, and comfort of the home, although they had not differed at intake in these skills.

Research Limitations

As with any study, there are flaws in the methodology that call for caution in interpreting results. While there was a fairly rigorous search for children and families in determining placement outcomes, there are families that may have been overlooked, especially more socially isolated families at higher risk of placement. The success rates should therefore be considered to be high estimates of prevented placements.

There is a possible confounding of family risks, resources, and stressors, simply because the same worker rated all of these things. While this evaluation hypothesized that family stressors and resources would be negatively correlated, the fact that the same worker rated all of these things may have clouded the evaluation's ability to judge these items independently. Supervisors do check workers' ratings of family progress and services periodically and also accompany workers to families' homes occasionally, so ratings were assumed to be fairly unbiased, but this was not directly assessed.

The majority of families in this study (99%) had housing and only 12% reported substance abuse. The problems of substance abuse and homelessness have increased alarmingly since 1987, and the program's ability to deal effectively with these problems has not been sufficiently addressed, due to the levels present in this study. An increasing proportion of families served are drug-affected, and continuing evaluation efforts will examine program effectiveness with this population.[3]

Conclusions

There are indeed some key factors to consider in the prediction of treatment success for an individual family. The family demographic characteristics that were examined did not vary greatly across all families in the sample, in that the majority of families were headed by a young single mother, were of low socioeconomic status, and had either two or three children, usually under the age of 5. Therefore, given the homogeneity of the sample, few demographic characteristics were associated with program success. Families that remained intact did have greater economic resources to draw on, however, and mothers in intact families were significantly older.

The stressors facing these families were many. Almost a third of families had experienced prior removals of one or more children. While almost all families had housing, about a fifth of families did not have a phone in their home, and 14% did not have food in the home at the intake visit. The majority of families received Medi-Cal and/or AFDC, with an average monthly income of $572 including AFDC payments, well under the poverty level. Families were rated by workers to be functioning poorly, on average, although parental capacity to be involved in treatment was fairly high. Placement risk levels of these families were judged by workers to be fairly high, but were lower among those families who had more economic and social resources.

The family's mental capacity to participate in service is a significant contributor to treatment success. When family members are developmentally disabled or otherwise mentally impaired, child placement is more likely despite equivalent service provision and equivalent skill gains during treatment. Child neglect is more likely among these families, and, again, child neglect was not strongly ameliorated by this program.

Program success varied with the presenting problem of the family. When the family's problem was deemed to be an environmental or economic one, or when it was one of physical handicap or illness, the Emergency Family Care program was fairly effective in preventing child placement. These successes reflect the ecological and resource-building focus of the program and the effectiveness of resource acquisition in ameliorating environmental, economic, and health problems. When the family's presenting problem was instead one of child neglect, child abuse, or parent substance abuse, however, the program was less successful, indicating the more pervasive and subtle effects of these types of parenting problems.

The availability of friends and relatives was found to contribute to the likelihood of placement in this analysis. Although relatives are usually thought to provide social and economic support, the presence of relatives in this study was a particularly strong predictor of subsequent child placement. This finding may indicate that relatives are also likely to report the incidence of child abuse or neglect, relatives are more likely to be a placement resource for families at risk, or that these relatives require the economic and social support of the identified family, rather than the other way around. These relatives may be a stressor rather than a resource, and the same can be said of the friends of families in the program. The nature of friends' and relatives' "help" was not addressed in the records available to this study, and should be addressed in subsequent data collection.

There are several service components that do make a difference. This analysis found that an average of 2½ months of service was effective in helping families at risk to remain intact (although their degree of risk is variable). The average family received 67 hours of service (about 9 hours a week), and more than a third of service time was spent in the home. This analysis indicates that while the total length of time the family is served is not related to outcome, the proportion of time that is spent *in the home* is highly related to success. Families that received larger proportions of their service time in the home were more likely to stay together.

In addition to a home focus, the type of service provided made a difference in outcome. Families were best served and more likely to remain intact when services were particularly concrete, such as the teaching of family care, supplemental parenting, medical care, helping in the securing of food, and financial services. These services were associated with parents making the greatest gains in skills and in families remaining intact after leaving the program. Also, when services had involved formal social supports, such as talklines, day care, respite care, and health care, families were more likely to stay together.

These findings demonstrate that short-term services can be effective when they include concrete services and the mobilization of resources. Families who received training in parenting and family care were quite successful in remaining a family. More informal support, especially when it involves friends and relatives, is not as effective with this population. The support of friends and relatives was detrimental to family stability both at intake and when they were enlisted to help as a part of treatment.

The skill gains that were associated with placement prevention were also more concrete than is usually addressed. Improvements in the cleanliness and overall condition of the living unit and in health care and encouragement of child development were significantly correlated with placement prevention, while gains in general child care and child discipline were not. Also, when clients continued to make gains in the cleanliness and condition of the living unit after the case was closed, families were much more likely to keep their children. These physical conditions are very visible and tangible indicators of the family environment, and influence placement decisions.

This study does not answer the question of whether families improved because of concrete services or because families in need of only concrete services were most easily served. More research is needed assessing the relative effectiveness of concrete and soft services, and the role of concrete and soft "outcomes" in influencing placement decisions following treatment. This study also does not address the issue of possible reabuse in a preserved family. Family care workers, in the course of conducting the 1-month, 6-month, and 1-year follow-up visits, were often the reporting party in cases of suspected child abuse and neglect following treatment, but this study did not specifically measure reabuse or neglect rates (but is measuring reabuse in current evaluation efforts).

The finding that services were less intensive and less effective among families referred for child neglect raises some interesting questions around the definition of the target population for family preservation services. Neglectful families have often taken a long time to develop into a crisis state, and will probably experience multiple crises on their road to preservation. It is very likely that 6 to 8 weeks of intensive assistance will need to be followed by "booster shot" services or periodic reenrollment in full services (Yuan & Struckman-Johnson, 1991).

The Children's Home Society program was created in 1980 to handle cases at imminent risk of placement by the Department of Social Services. However, this public/private agency collaboration around placement prevention necessitates much better delineation of decision-making factors around placement by DSS and communication of those key placement risk factors to the Children's Home Society program, if placement prevention is the key outcome. If improvement of family functioning is the key outcome, then family functioning should carry more weight in the placement decision by DSS.

Because family preservation programs are aimed at preventing placement, and because the decision to remove a child is often associated with economic indicators rather than severity of maltreatment (Lindsey, 1991; Pelton, 1989), the outcome of placement may or may not be directly impacted by changing parenting practices or improving family relations. It may be that improving economic conditions and environmental indicators of safety and orderliness will have the greatest impact on reducing risk of placement, because these physical, visual indicators of family functioning are the most dramatic indicators of maltreatment.

Some family preservation programs recognize the importance of these physical and economic factors by providing flexible funds of $100 to $500 per case, with which in-home workers can improve economic or environmental conditions by installing a phone, repairing the car, or buying a child's bed, without making such an expenditure fit into some billable category of service. This illustrates a recognition of the contribution of the physical environment to family functioning and the placement decision. Granted, improving the home environment should benefit both physical and emotional well-being, but the current focus of child welfare services purely on investigation and child protection will continue to create a tension in family preservation programs between the utility of different types of helping (improving family functioning vs. prevention of placement).

If family preservation programs are mandated to serve their defined target population of families in crisis, then they must be viewed as part of a larger array of economic and parenting supports for all families (Yuan & Struckman-Johnson, 1991). Programs that hope to reduce unnecessary placement without addressing systemic decision making around placement may do best by focusing on improving economic resources, job skills, and environmental/physical indicators that will influence those placement decisions. This begs the larger question of the appropriateness of placement for such families.

Notes

1. Copies of the assessment and tracking forms are available from the author at the University of Texas at Arlington School of Social Work, P.O. Box 19129, Arlington, Texas, 76019.

2. All *t* tests in this study were examined for unequal sample variances, due to fluctuating sample sizes, and separate variance estimates are reported when appropriate.

3. Results of an evaluation of services to drug-affected families are available from the author.

References

Allen, M. (1990, Spring). Why are we talking about case management again? *The Prevention Report*, pp. 1-2.

American Humane Association. (1988). *Highlights of official child neglect and abuse reporting, 1986.* Denver: Author.

AuClaire, P., & Schwartz, I. M. (1986). *An evaluation of the effectiveness of intensive home-based services as an alternative to placement for adolescents and their families.* Minneapolis: University of Minnesota, Hubert H. Humphrey Institute of Public Affairs.

Barth, R. P. (1990). Theories guiding home-based intensive family preservation services. In J. K. Whittaker, J. Kinney, E. M. Tracy, & C. Booth (Eds.), *Reaching high-risk families: Intensive family preservation in human services.* Hawthorne, NY: Aldine de Gruyter.

Behavioral Sciences Institute. (1987). *Summary of King, Pierce, Snohomish, and Spokane county Homebuilders service, September 1, 1986-August 31, 1987.* Federal Way, WA: Author.

Belle, D. (1982). Social ties and social support. In D. Belle (Ed.), *Lives in stress: Women and depression.* Beverly Hills, CA: Sage.

Berry, M. (1991). The assessment of imminence of risk of placement: Lessons from a family preservation program. *Children and Youth Services Review, 13,* 239-256.

Berry, M. (1992). An evaluation of family preservation services: Fitting agency services to family needs. *Social Work, 37,* 314-321.

Cochran, M. M., & Brassard, J. A. (1979). Child development and personal social networks. *Child Development, 50,* 601-616.

Friedman, R. M. (1976). Child abuse: A review of the psychosocial research. In Herner and Company (Eds.), *Four perspectives on the status of child abuse and neglect research.* Washington, DC: National Center on Child Abuse and Neglect.

Gaines, R., Sandgrund, A., Green, A. H., & Power, E. (1978). Etiological factors in child maltreatment: A multivariate study of abusing, neglecting and normal mothers. *Journal of Abnormal Psychology, 87,* 531-540.

Garbarino, J. (1976). A preliminary study of some ecological correlates of child abuse: The impact of socioeconomic stress on mothers. *Child Development, 47,* 178-185.

Garbarino, J. (1977). The human ecology of child maltreatment: A conceptual model for research. *Journal of Marriage and the Family, 39,* 721-735.

Garbarino, J. (1981). An ecological approach to child maltreatment. In L. H. Pelton (Ed.), *The social context of child abuse and neglect.* New York: Human Sciences Press.

Gil, D. G. (1973). *Violence against children: Physical child abuse in the United States.* Cambridge, MA: Harvard University Press.

Johnson, W., & L'Esperance, J. (1984). Predicting the recurrence of child abuse. *Social Work Research and Abstracts, 20,* 21-31.

Kamerman, S. B., & Kahn, A. J. (1989). *Social services for children, youth and families in the United States.* Ann Arbor, MI: The Annie E. Casey Foundation.

Katz, M. H., Hampton, R. L., Newberger, E. H., Bowles, R. T., & Snyder, J. C. (1986). Returning children home: Clinical decision making in cases of child abuse and neglect. *American Journal of Orthopsychiatry, 56,* 253-263.

Kinney, J., Haapala, D. A., Booth, C., & Leavitt, S. (1988). The homebuilders model. In J. K. Whittaker, J. Kinney, E. M. Tracy, & C. Booth (Eds.), *Improving practice technology for work with high risk families: Lessons from the "Homebuilders" social work education project.* Seattle: University of Washington School of Social Work Center for Social Welfare Research.

Landsman, M. J. (1985). *Evaluation of fourteen child placement prevention projects in Wisconsin, 1983-1985.* Iowa City, IA: University of Iowa, National Resource Center on Family Based Services.

Lindsey, D. (1991). Factors affecting the foster care placement decision: An analysis of national survey data. *American Journal of Orthopsychiatry, 61*(2), 272-281.

Lovell, M. L., & Hawkins, J. D. (1988). An evaluation of a group intervention to increase the personal social networks of abusive mothers. *Children and Youth Services Review, 10,* 175-188.

Magura, S., & Moses, B. S. (1986). *Outcome measures for child welfare services: Theory and applications.* Washington, DC: Child Welfare League of America.

Maluccio, A. N., & Whittaker, J. K. (1988). Helping the biological families of children in out-of-home placement. In E. W. Nunnally, C. S. Chilman, & F. M. Cox (Eds.), *Families in trouble: Troubled relationships.* Beverly Hills, CA: Sage.

McClelland, D. (1973). Testing for competence rather than intelligence. *American Psychologist, 28,* 1-14.

Nelson, K. E. (1991). Populations and outcomes in five family preservation programs. In K. Wells & D. E. Biegel (Eds.), *Family preservation services: Research and evaluation.* Newbury Park, CA: Sage.

Parke, R., & Collmer, C. W. (1975). Child abuse: An interdisciplinary analysis. In E. M. Hetherington (Ed.), *Review of child developmental research* (Vol. 5). Chicago: University of Chicago Press.

Patterson, G. R. (1980). Mothers: The unacknowledged victims. *Monographs of the Society for Research in Child Development, 45*(5), 1-64.

Patterson, G. R. (1982). *Coercive family process.* Eugene, OR: Castalia.

Paulson, M. J., Afifi, A. A., Chaleff, A., Liu, V. Y., & Thomason, M. L. (1975). A discriminant function procedure for identifying abusive parents. *Suicide, 5,* 104-114.

Pecora, P. (1988). Evaluating risk assessment systems: Methodological issues and selected research findings. In P. Schene & K. Bond (Ed.), *Research issues in risk assessment for child protection.* Denver: American Association for Protecting Children.

Pecora, P. J., Fraser, M. W., Haapala, D. A., & Bartlomé, J. A. (1987). *Defining family preservation services: Three intensive home-based treatment programs.* Salt Lake City: University of Utah Social Research Institute.

Pelton, L. H. (1989). *For reasons of poverty: An evaluation of child welfare policy.* New York: Praeger.

Polansky, N. A. (1976). Analysis of research on child neglect: The social work viewpoint. In Herner and Company (Eds.), *Four perspectives on the status of child abuse and neglect research.* Washington, DC: National Center on Child Abuse and Neglect.

Polansky, N. A., & Gaudin, J. M. (1983). Social distancing of the neglectful family. *Social Service Review, 57,* 196-208.

Reid, W. J., Kagan, R. M., & Schlosberg, S. B. (1988). Prevention of placement: Critical factors in program success. *Child Welfare, 67,* 25-36.

Remy, L. L., & Hanson, S. P. (1982). *Evaluation of the emergency family care program, San Francisco Home Health Service: The basic evaluation.* San Francisco: San Francisco Home Health Service.

Remy, L. L., & Hanson, S. P. (1983). *Evaluation of the emergency family care program, San Francisco Home Health Service: Final report.* San Francisco: San Francisco Home Health Service.

Saulnier, K. M., & Rowland, C. (1985). Missing links: An empirical investigation of network variables in high risk families. *Family Relations, 34,* 557-560.

Shapiro, D. (1980). A CWLA study of factors involved in child abuse. *Child Welfare, 59,* 242-243.

Showell, W. H. (1985). *1983-1985 biennial report of CSD's intensive family services.* Salem: State of Oregon Children's Services Division.

Showell, W. H., Hartley, R., & Allen, M. (1987). *Outcomes of Oregon's family therapy programs: A descriptive study of 999 families.* Salem: State of Oregon Children's Services Division.

Spinetta, J. J., & Rigler, D. (1972). The child-abusing parent: A psychological review. *Psychological Bulletin, 77,* 296-304.

Stehno, S. (1986). Family-centered child welfare services: New life for a historic idea. *Child Welfare, 65,* 231-240.

Tracy, E. M. (1990). Identifying social support resources of at-risk families. *Social Work, 35,* 252-258.

Tracy, E. M. (1991). Defining the target population for family preservation services. In K. Wells & D. E. Biegel (Eds.), *Family preservation services: Research and evaluation.* Newbury Park, CA: Sage.

Van Meter, M. J. S., Haynes, O. M., & Kropp, J. P. (1987). The negative social work network: When friends are foes. *Child Welfare, 66,* 69-75.

Wahler, R. G., & Dumas, J. E. (1984). Changing the observational coding styles of insular and noninsular mothers: A step toward maintenance of parent training effects. In R. F. Dangel & R. A. Polster (Eds.), *Parent training: Foundations of research and practice.* New York: Guilford.

Whittaker, J. K., Schinke, S. P., & Gilchrist, L. D. (1986). The ecological paradigm in child, youth, and family services: Implications for policy and practice. *Social Service Review, 60,* 483-503.

Yuan, Y.-Y. T., & Struckman-Johnson, D. L. (1991). Placement outcomes for neglected children with prior placements in family preservation programs. In K. Wells & D. E. Biegel (Eds.), *Family preservation services: Research and evaluation.* Newbury Park, CA: Sage.

7

Shifting Objectives in Family Preservation Programs

JULIA H. LITTELL
JOHN R. SCHUERMAN
TINA L. RZEPNICKI
JEANNE HOWARD
STEPHEN BUDDE

There is a widening gap between the placement prevention objective and informal, widely held goals for intensive family preservation programs. The original intent of family preservation programs was to prevent the out-of-home placement of children by providing intensive services to families in the hope that these services would correct conditions in the home that might lead to placement. We suggest that the purpose of these programs has been broadened informally to include the provision of services for families that do not have children who are at risk of placement but who need immediate, intensive, and concrete services that are not readily available elsewhere. Some program advocates argue that intensive family preservation services can have important benefits for children and families, regardless of whether placement is imminent. It is the goal of this chapter to consider how this shift in

AUTHORS' NOTE: The authors are grateful for the assistance of Amy Chak, Brenda Eckhardt, Mark Hugel, Penny Johnson, Diane Pellowe, Sandra Rick, and Katherine Bernadette Smith, who conducted interviews and contributed to the development of this chapter. Funding for the evaluation of the Illinois Family First program was provided by the Illinois Department of Children and Family Services.

program objectives has come about, as well as the implications of this shift on current thinking about the effects of these programs. We pay particular attention to the problem of targeting placement prevention programs; we suggest that this problem has contributed to shifts in program objectives.

Our observations are drawn from a large-scale evaluation of the family preservation program in Illinois. The Illinois program, known as Family First, is one of the largest of its kind. It covers the entire state, operating through contracts between the state child welfare department (the Department of Children and Family Services, DCFS) and 59 private agencies. Family First serves families with children under age 13 who are thought to be at risk of removal from their homes because of child abuse and neglect. Like other family preservation programs, Family First provides immediate, intensive services for families in their homes.[1] The evaluation of this program includes an experiment involving the random assignment of families to Family First or to a control group receiving the regular services of the Department of Children and Family Services (DCFS).

Background

The Adoption Assistance and Child Welfare Act of 1980 (P.L. 96-272) stipulated that states must make "reasonable efforts" to prevent out-of-home placement in cases of child abuse and neglect. This legislation reflected years of concern about problems in foster care and research on the importance of attachment between parents and children that suggested that a "bad" home may be better for children than a "good" institution (Bowlby, 1951; Maluccio & Fein, 1985). Rising foster care caseloads and media stories and class action suits regarding children who were taken out of their homes for apparently trivial reasons—often because the family lacked resources that could have been provided for them—were seen by child advocates as evidence that many out-of-home placements were unnecessary.

Early studies of the effects of family preservation programs focused on the Homebuilders model, a program of brief, intensive, in-home services developed in Tacoma, Washington, in the late 1970s.[2] The results of these studies were quite favorable: They suggested that placement could be avoided in 85%-90% of the cases. Based on this evidence, family preservation programs were developed and are now flourishing in a number of states. Their stated purpose: to prevent unnecessary out-of-home placements.

It should be noted that the assumptions that many placements are unnecessary and that many placements can be prevented by family preservation programs are not well supported by existing research. First, there has been little systematic research on how placement decisions are made, the factors affecting these decisions, and the extent to which "unnecessary" placements occur. Second, early studies of the effects of family preservation programs were marred by serious methodological flaws; more rigorous studies have called into question the earlier findings of large placement prevention effects.

Early evaluations of family preservation programs lacked adequate control groups. In these studies, it was assumed that virtually all program families would have experienced placement of a child in the absence of the program. Thus, if 15% of the program families experienced placement, this was seen as a "placement prevention rate" of 85%. Studies employing true control groups have found that the proportion of family preservation cases that would have experienced placement in the absence of these programs is actually rather small.[3] A randomized study of intensive family preservation programs in New Jersey found that 15% of control group cases involved placement within 6 weeks after referral (Feldman, 1990). A similar study in California found that placement had occurred in 20% of control group cases within 8 months (McDonald & Associates, 1990).[4] Preliminary results from the randomized evaluation of family preservation programs in Illinois show that approximately 8% of control group cases involve placement within the first month (Chapin Hall Center, 1991). Because the risk of placement among these families is so low, program effects on placement may be quite difficult to detect; it is likely that there is a "ceiling" on these effects.[5]

Rigorous evaluations have also provided little evidence that family preservation programs affect placement rates for the relatively small proportion of families who are at risk of placement. In New Jersey, intensive family preservation programs appeared to delay—but not prevent—placements: program families were significantly less likely than control group families to experience placement between 1 and 9 months after referral; however, after one year the differences between these groups were no longer significant (Feldman, 1990).[6] In California, family preservation cases were slightly more likely to involve placement than those in the control group, although this finding was not statistically significant (McDonald & Associates, 1990).[7] Preliminary results from the Illinois experiment show no significant differences in placement rates between program and control groups.[8]

Why aren't family preservation programs getting the "right" kinds of referrals (families at risk of placement)? and why don't they seem to reduce the risk of placement? We suggest that part of the answer to these questions is that the goals for these programs have been broadened beyond placement prevention.

Diverse Interests

Like most social service programs, family preservation programs have many stakeholders who have been influential in their development and implementation. In Illinois, these interest groups include state child welfare administrators, child protection investigators, private agency administrators, private agency workers, advocacy groups, professional associations, advisory boards, and the state legislature. At the national level, several foundations (notably the Edna McConnell Clark Foundation and the Annie E. Casey Foundation), congressional committees, and federal agencies are involved in the development of family preservation programs. Although these stakeholders share an interest in preventing unnecessary placements and improving the quality of services available for families and children, they have different perspectives on the appropriate means and ends of the family preservation programs. To begin with, the stakeholders have quite different views of how program "success" should be defined.

Policy goals. The legislative authority for the Family First program is provided by the Illinois Family Preservation Act. The goals of this Act are to "prevent the placement of children in substitute care." In Illinois, as in other states, support for family preservation services in the state legislature has been based on the following assumptions: (a) children are often better off in their own homes than in foster care, (b) a substantial number of unnecessary placements are being made, and (c) family preservation services will result in a substantial savings in foster care costs.

The formal goals of the Illinois Family First program are not confined to placement prevention. In 1988, the DCFS request for proposals for family preservation services stated that these services were intended to:

1. Increase the accessibility of services for abusive or neglectful families.

2. Establish a comprehensive range of services that assess the risk of harm to children while responding to the immediate and long-term needs of referred families.
3. Increase the family's level of functioning to prevent the reoccurrence of abuse or neglect.
4. Increase the use of community-based services to support the family and prevent the placement of children (Illinois Department of Children and Family Services, 1988, p. 12).

The outcome goals for this program were stated as follows:

85% of the families who were intact at the time of the referral will remain intact during the service period and for a period of six (6) months following the termination of services;

80% of the families served will not be the subjects of indicated reports of abuse or neglect during the service period and for a period of six (6) months following the termination of services;

90% of the families referred will receive at least one service through a community provider via a linkage or referral initiated by the awardee;

100% of the families referred will have face-to-face contact with the agency within 24 hours of the agency's receipt of the referral;

80% of the families referred will receive services which alleviate the symptoms that brought the family to the attention of the Department (Illinois Department of Children and Family Services, 1988, p. 13).

Other goals of program planners. Our interviews with program planners in DCFS and the state's Child Welfare Advisory Committee indicate that some of the original architects of the Family First program were concerned exclusively with preventing unnecessary placements. They saw family preservation programs as a remedy for serious problems in substitute care, including rising foster care caseloads, overcrowding in temporary shelters, and maltreatment of children in the foster care system. Others were concerned more generally about the lack of services available to families in the public child welfare system; they saw the placement prevention rhetoric as a means to improve the quality of services available for these families. For the latter group of program planners, family preservation programs provided an avenue for rebuilding basic social services within a framework that was politically attractive (because it focused on strengthening families and reducing state intervention) and—presumably—cost effective.

The Family First program has been seen—by both DCFS and private agency staff—as a means of transferring responsibility for child protective services from DCFS to the private agencies. Many government officials and private agency executives believe that the private sector can provide better quality services for these families and that the private agencies should assume more responsibility for child welfare services. Some private agencies have also seen the Family First program as a means to acquire funding for services that they already provide.

The goals of DCFS line staff. Initially, some child protection investigators hoped that Family First would reduce their workload by shifting the responsibility for risk assessment and court appearances to private agency workers. A more commonly held view is that the program provides child protection investigators with a way to handle uncertain situations in which decisions regarding the case disposition are difficult (e.g., cases in which placement may be necessary but further documentation of abuse or neglect is required, and cases in which further assessment is needed in order to determine the level of risk to children). Similarly, some DCFS staff have seen Family First as a way to reduce the caseloads of public child welfare caseworkers. In some regions the program is also seen as a means to accelerate access to services and expedite case closings.

In general, DCFS staff are more concerned about child protection issues (their primary goal is protecting children), while private agency staff tend to focus on a wider range of concerns related to the functioning of the children's primary caregivers (their primary goal is helping parents). DCFS staff also place greater emphasis on the provision of concrete services, while some (not all) private agency staff see these things as "Band-Aids" and believe that advocacy and counseling services are more important.[9]

The goals of private agency staff. Our interviews with private agency staff who are involved in providing family preservation services to families suggest that these workers focus on process goals (such as reaching the family quickly, assessing the risk of harm to children, identifying other family problems) and immediate outcomes (including acquiring concrete services for the family, improving the caregiver's parenting skills, and placing children when necessary). Line staff's views of the benefits of the program other than placement prevention will be explored in more detail in a later section. We wish to note here that workers often report that a case was a "success" because they did what they were supposed to do—they met the family within the first 24 hours, provided in-home and concrete services, and engaged the family in intervention efforts—even if there was no improvement or some deterioration in the family's situation.[10]

Another important aspect of private agency staff views of program objectives is that they see the aim of their work as "helping families"— in whatever ways are necessary. Since families' needs are diverse, measures of success can vary from one family to another. In some workers' views, the Family First program is successful because it provides a flexible array of immediate and intensive services that can be tailored to a particular family's needs. In this view, virtually any policy goals (such as placement prevention) and aggregate measures of success are less relevant than families' progress toward the achievement of individualized goals. This reflects a general tension between policy goals, which prescribe generalized changes in a target group, and treatment goals, which tend to be highly individualized.

Changes in objectives over time. The implementation of social programs is often accompanied by an accretion of goals as program planners attempt to satisfy diverse interest groups. Service providers often believe that their efforts have important benefits in addition to the original goals of the program and that their services are appropriate for a wider target population. Certainly, this is the case in the Illinois Family First program.

We have also noted changes over time in the ways in which program objectives have been conceptualized. Social programs are rarely implemented as originally planned. During the implementation phase, goals are often adjusted as program staff discover the real constraints on their work. The original goals may have been unrealistic or inappropriate (placement prevention may not be possible or desirable in many cases). Midcourse corrections are often needed.[11] Revised expectations, based on some experience with the program, may be more realistic than the original goals.

Program administrators sometimes attempt to modify the original intent of the program (e.g., by allowing the referral of cases that are not at risk of placement or by relaxing a "no decline" policy).[12] They may focus on process rather than outcome goals (e.g., attempted contacts versus actual contacts with families), since the former are easier to achieve.[13] Legislators and administrators should be aware of such shifts (the identification of shifts in program objectives is one of the functions of program evaluation) and must determine whether the new goals serve important social values.

The Various Objectives of Placement Prevention Programs

Many objectives for family preservation programs have been suggested in our discussions with public and private agency staff. In this section, we explore these objectives further.

Benefits for Children

It is often suggested that family preservation programs should result in improvements in such things as children's health, school performance, and social skills. These effects are generally thought to be indirect in that they usually come about because of changes in parents, who are the focus of intervention in this program. There are few interventions that are directly aimed at children in the Family First placement prevention program.[14]

Child protection. A central idea in family preservation programs is that by altering conditions related to risk of abuse or neglect there may be a reduction in the likelihood of subsequent substantiated reports of harm. Whether or not that happens, children may be better protected when workers make frequent home visits. This increased monitoring (or surveillance) may inhibit child maltreatment. In other cases, enhanced monitoring and assessment may lead to the identification of abuse or neglect that might not have been detected had the family preservation worker not been involved in the case. This "case finding" activity may increase the likelihood of subsequent reports of child maltreatment and may lead to placement in some cases.

Better placements. The program may result in better planning for placement, so that the "right" children are placed, parents are more willing to accept foster care placement, visitation occurs frequently, and parents are better prepared for the child's return home. This may result in shorter or more stable placements. There also may be a greater number of appropriate placements with relatives. Relative placements keep children closer to home and may provide parents with better access to their children (for better or worse). Skeptics might argue that the retrospective reconstruction of placement cases (as "better" or "worse" than something else) is questionable: It can always be argued that these placements are somehow "better" than those that would have been made in the absence of the program.

Benefits for Families

Family preservation programs are said to have a wide range of benefits for families. Some of these are explored below.

Better assessments. Family preservation programs may result in better identification and understanding of family problems and, therefore, more appropriate service provision. Family preservation workers acquire a great deal of information about conditions in the home, the nature of family strengths and problems, and risks to children. Much of this information may not be available to other child welfare workers.

Greater involvement of clients. Some family preservation programs may be able to involve clients in problem identification (assessment) and service planning more successfully than regular child welfare services can. Greater client involvement in assessment and planning may be related to higher levels of cooperation with service providers and better outcomes.

Enhanced family functioning. Enhanced family functioning is an objective expressed by many family preservation workers. For them, program success means that families are better off as a result of the intervention, whether or not placement occurs. *Family functioning* covers a multitude of things. Workers are interested in seeing parents take more responsibility for their children and they are concerned about improving intrafamilial relationships, clarifying roles, and improving communication.

When workers talk about their efforts to improve family functioning, they often stress the notion that these goals must be highly individualized. There is a great deal of variation among the families in these programs—in the problems they face, their strengths, and their skills in negotiating the service system—thus, workers focus on reduction of case-specific problems. We identify here some of these individualized goals.

Family preservation programs may result in improved parenting skills. Parents may learn more effective and less harmful discipline techniques, how to show affection, how to take care of children's physical needs (nutrition, health care), and how to understand and meet children's social and emotional needs.

Resolution or reduction of intrafamilial conflicts may occur through informal and formal counseling. Workers sometimes focus on clarifying familial roles, particularly when confusion or boundary problems exist (e.g., when a grandmother is interfering in the mother-child relationship). Improved communication between family members is another goal that some family preservation workers express.

Some workers emphasize their efforts to "empower" caregivers and older children. Workers attempt to increase clients' self-confidence and help them develop a sense that they have the power to change their life circumstances. In addition, workers often try to improve clients' problem-solving and negotiating skills. As a result, clients may demonstrate increased willingness to express needs, seek services, and negotiate with public agency workers. This may lead to improvements in clients' abilities to seek and find social support from friends and relatives. It may result in increased demands for services in some cases and in reduced dependency on social welfare programs in others.

Improvements in the home environment may be made that ameliorate unsafe or unsanitary conditions. Clients may also develop the knowledge and skills needed to negotiate with landlords and utility companies and to create a safer environment for their children.

Better "linkage" to community services. Most family preservation programs are expected to make use of referrals to other community agencies for services. They may do a better job (than "regular" child welfare services can) in helping clients establish relationships with other service providers by accompanying clients to service agencies and making sure clients follow through with referrals.

When family preservation workers monitor referrals carefully, they may detect situations in which the referral is not really what the client needs (e.g., the program is not what it's cracked up to be, the client is on a long waiting list, or the client is not happy with the service) and the worker can then take corrective action by helping the client seek other services. This might result in "better" referrals.

Family preservation programs may increase clients' knowledge about resources that are available in their community. This may help to prepare families to handle future crises better. It may also increase the likelihood that clients will receive counseling, get into drug treatment programs, find work, or receive public aid after they have left the family preservation program. These services may in turn have important benefits for clients. Enhanced knowledge of community resources and better linkages may also increase clients' sense of connectedness to the community and reduce social isolation.

Faster case closings. In Illinois there are marked regional variations in expectations about whether family preservation programs should divert families from the child welfare system. In some areas, these programs are expected to result in quicker case closings by resolving the problems that bring families into contact with child protective services. In other regions, the programs are thought to have no effect or to delay case closing. Some workers suggest that some families may remain in the child welfare system longer because family preservation programs develop additional information about clients' problems and service needs.

Systemic Effects

Family preservation programs may encourage a family-centered orientation in other parts of the child welfare and social service systems. These programs may affect the attitudes and beliefs of public child welfare workers and the ways in which these workers attempt to balance the dual—and sometimes conflicting—goals of child protection and family preservation in cases that are not involved in family preservation programs.

When private child welfare agencies are involved in the provision of family preservation services, these programs are also likely to have important effects on the private agencies. The family preservation orientation may result in lasting changes in casework practices, perceptions of families' needs, and the nature of the agencies' clientele. These programs may encourage the provision of in-home, intensive, short-term, and concrete services to families—representing an important change in modality for some service providers. Family preservation programs may promote an emphasis on practical problem-solving strategies to meet families' immediate needs. They may encourage private agency staff to work with low-income multiproblem families and protective service cases (these are new target populations for some private child welfare agencies).

In Illinois the Family First program has increased available funding for some private child welfare services. This may result in the development of a new interest group (family preservation service providers) that may work to maintain the new status quo (maintain funding) regardless of whether the new program meets its objectives. The Illinois Family First program may also encourage cooperation between public and private child welfare agencies. Closer cooperation may result in better case planning and smoother delivery of services to families.

Finally, many types of services are now more readily available to families served by the public child welfare system—including cash and other concrete assistance, homemaking services, and in-home assessments and counseling—as a result of family preservation programs. These programs may also serve to document shortages of certain services in specific geographic areas.

The Problem of Targeting

There are special problems involved in mounting and evaluating programs that are designed to prevent certain events from occurring (regardless of whether the event of interest is teenage pregnancy, child abuse, out-of-home placement, delinquency, or drug abuse). It seems evident that such "prevention programs" ought to serve people who are likely to experience the event of interest (in our case, the placement of one or more children) in the absence of the program. This requires an assessment of whether or not people are likely to experience the event in the future. The ability of human service professionals to predict such events accurately is limited. As a result, targeting is likely to be inexact: Some families referred to family preservation programs might have experienced placement in the absence of these programs, while others would not.[15]

As with other social programs, it is possible that the size of the target population for family preservation programs has been overestimated. Family preservation programs will fail to meet the placement prevention objective when they are poorly targeted: If few of the families who are referred to these programs would have experienced placement in the absence of these services, it is unlikely that the programs will be able to demonstrate a "placement prevention effect."

Beyond identifying cases at risk of placement, referral agents should identify families who are most likely to benefit from these programs. Thus, for targeting to be effective, it must be possible to separate cases that are likely to succeed from those that are not.[16] This requires (a) the identification of factors critical to case success or failure, (b) the availability of measures of those factors, and (c) the ability to measure critical factors at the time of referral. As with the prediction of future placement, the prediction of success or failure is quite problematic. For example, one of the factors that may be critical to success is the client's motivation to change, including the family's willingness to acknowledge problems and its level of involvement in services. It may be impossible to measure these characteristics at the time of referral, since "motivation" often develops out of the relationship between a client and worker. Families who appear to be motivated at the onset may be putting on a facade, while initial resistance in others may be overcome. Thus the conditions for success may appear or develop only in the process of working with a family. These conditions may also have to do with certain qualities of the worker (e.g., enthusiasm; skillful use of the helping relationship; establishing specificity and congruence regarding the identification of problems, goals, and appropriate intervention strategies) or the quality of the interaction (or "fit") between the worker and client.

It may be possible at the time of referral to identify a group of cases that are clearly unlikely to succeed (for example, parents who have rejected all responsibility for the child, cases in which children have experienced life-threatening injury at the hands of a parent who shows no remorse) and a group that is highly likely to succeed, but both of those groups are probably relatively small. A large "middle" group will be left in which the likelihood of success is unclear. There are two possible responses to this situation. One is to restrict the program to those few cases in which the probability of success is known to be high at the time of referral. Programs would then be relatively small and many cases that might benefit would be excluded. Alternatively, some or all of the cases in the middle group could be served. Programs would then be larger and some resources would be devoted to families who will not benefit.

In any case, it may be very difficult to design an effective algorithm for specifying a target group of cases that are likely to benefit from family preservation programs. These limitations arise out of problems in the identification and measurement of factors that are critical to success at the time of referral.

Implications for Program Evaluation

The evaluation of any public program should (a) assess the extent to which the program attains formal, societal goals expressed in legislation and other governmental pronouncements, (b) document shifts and accretion of goals, and (c) examine (insofar as possible) the effects of the program beyond formal objectives—effects that society might be interested in promoting or suppressing. Evaluation issues that arise from our exploration of various objectives for family preservation programs are discussed below.

Using multiple measures. Outcome measures ought to be derived at least in part from formal and informal program objectives, although we suggest that evaluators and others may add new ways of thinking about program effects to the objectives articulated by policymakers and service providers. Changes in policymakers' and program providers' expectations of programs underscore the importance of incorporating multiple outcome measures in an evaluation. At a minimum, evaluations of family preservation programs ought to consider program effects on placement, subsequent harm to children, and measures of child and family functioning.[17]

Determining the durability of effects. Little attention has been paid to the durability of gains that result from social interventions (Rzepnicki, 1991). Longitudinal studies are needed to determine how long various effects last. It may be that gains in certain areas are more durable than others, and that follow-up services are needed to maintain certain benefits.

Measuring unintended consequences. Evaluators should always consider possible unintended negative effects of intervention programs, since these are usually not identified by program providers or advocates. Evaluations of family preservation programs must consider the possibility of increased risk of harm to children when they are left in their own homes. Other unintended negative consequences may include increased dependency of families on private and public agencies. (Programs that focus on establishing long-term relationships between workers and clients may encourage families to rely on service providers to meet their emotional needs.)

Examining systemic effects. Evaluators can explore systemic effects that have not been articulated by others. This includes examination of indirect effects of the program on other parts of the service delivery system, such as changes in ways of thinking about the balance between child protection and family preservation in child welfare services.

Getting the clients' views. There have been few systematic attempts to understand clients' views of family preservation programs. Clients' perspectives on the value of services to them are important in evaluating any social program. It is particularly important to understand clients' views of intensive—and possibly intrusive—service programs such as these, even if society believes that the intrusion is justified or necessary. We suggest that service providers may find it difficult to get clients' honest views of the program (consumer satisfaction surveys conducted by program providers are often unreliable), and therefore these views should be solicited by experienced outside evaluators.

Conclusions

We suggest that a shift in objectives for family preservation programs is taking place. The original goal of placement prevention is being shifted to broader efforts to enhance child and family functioning in protective services cases. How should this shift in objectives be reflected in evaluation of these programs?

In our view, the placement prevention objective should not be abandoned. It may turn out that some family preservation programs reduce the likelihood of placement in certain areas or under certain conditions (e.g., with better targeting or more intensive programs). On the other hand, there may be little that can be done to alter the need for placement in some cases. The testing of placement prevention effects and the documentation of conditions under which placement can be prevented are important tasks that have not yet been accomplished.

Even if placement prevention effects are not evident, other important benefits may be. Program evaluations should incorporate information from various stakeholders about what the program really can and should do for families.[18] Intensive family preservation programs may benefit children and families in many ways. Like any social program, they may also have positive and negative consequences that are unintended.

Notes

1. For a description of the Illinois Family First program, see Schuerman, Rzepnicki, and Littell (1990).

2. For a description of the Homebuilders model, see Kinney, Haapala, Booth, and Leavitt (1991).

3. In these studies, cases are randomly assigned to program and control groups. The two groups should be identical in all respects except that they receive different types of services. Thus the placement rates among control group cases can be thought of as the risk of placement for families in the family preservation programs, had they not received family preservation services.

4. Results of the New Jersey and California experiments and difficulties with the standard of "imminent risk of placement" are discussed by Nelson (1990).

5. It has been argued that randomized experiments may encourage referral of families who do not have children at risk of placement by increasing the number of referrals needed in order to fill program slots. If this were true, we would expect to find lower placement rates among families who entered the program in experimental sites after the beginning of an experiment. Our research indicates that there are no significant differences in the placement rates for families who entered the Illinois Family First program before and after the experiment began. We also found similar placement rates among program clients

in experimental and nonexperimental sites (Littell, Schuerman, & Rzepnicki, 1991). This suggests that in Illinois the conduct of a randomized experiment has not resulted in the referral of a smaller proportion of families with children at risk of placement.

6. Fifty-eight percent of families in the control group experienced placement within one year, compared with 46% of those in the family preservation programs, a statistically nonsignificant difference (Feldman, 1990).

7. Twenty-five percent of family preservation cases involved placement within 8 months after referral, compared with 20% of those in the control group (McDonald & Associates, 1990).

8. It is possible that significant differences between the placement rates of program and control groups will emerge in certain sites as this study grows larger. The numbers of cases in each of the seven sites in the study are too small at this time to detect program effects in specific sites.

9. Private agency staff often make a distinction between the provision of concrete services and teaching clients to acquire these services themselves. Many believe that the latter (advocacy efforts) are more important.

10. This has been termed *functional rationality,* that is, a concern with fairness, due process, and adherence to standard procedures, in contrast to *substantive rationality* in which the focus is on the effects of services on clients (Marshall, 1964).

11. In its 1988 request for proposals for family preservation services, DCFS noted that the "initial target goals . . . may be revised to reflect the results of the Family First evaluation and the provider's actual experience with the Initiative" (Illinois Department of Children and Family Services, 1988, p. 13).

12. Initially, Family First providers had to accept referrals on a no-decline basis as part of their contract with DCFS. This rule was intended to prevent service providers from rejecting difficult cases. Over time, and as working relationships between referral agents and service providers developed, service providers found ways to influence referral decisions. Some were successful in avoiding referrals of certain kinds of cases (e.g., families with housing or cocaine problems). In some areas, the no-decline policy was eventually amended, so that a service provider could reject a case within the first seven days of service.

13. One of the original goals of the Family First program was to establish in-person contact with family members within the first 24 hours of service. Service providers found that some families could not be reached within this time frame (some families had moved, were not at home, or avoided contact with the worker). Many argued that the focus should be on whether the Family First worker *attempted* contact with the family within 24 hours of referral.

14. Direct effects on children may include enrollment in school, vaccinations, preventive medical care, and improvement in social and psychological functioning.

15. This is also the case in home health care programs designed to prevent institutionalization. Weissert, Cready, and Pawelak (1988) reviewed results of 27 experiments or quasi experiments on the effects of home and community care. They conclude that "home care is not a cost-saving substitute for nursing home care because few patients are at risk of institutionalization; reductions in institutionalization are small; home care costs exceed the small reductions in institutional costs; and patient outcome benefits are extremely limited, and sometimes even negative" (p. 175).

16. Note that there are many definitions of case "success" that could be applied here. At a minimum, we suggest that success means that the safety of children can be protected with in-home services; that is, that there are no further incidents of child abuse or neglect. A more common definition of case success is that, in addition to lack of further incidents of child maltreatment, there is some improvement in conditions in the home related to children's safety and well-being.

17. For a more complete discussion of issues in the evaluation of family preservation programs see Schuerman, Rzepnicki, and Littell (1991), Rzepnicki, Schuerman, and Littell (1991), and Yuan and Rivest (1990).

18. This is one of the reasons we frequently interview program administrators and line staff.

References

Bowlby, J. (1951). *Maternal care and mental health.* Geneva: World Health Organization.

Chapin Hall Center for Children. (1991, June). *Evaluation of the Illinois Department of Children and Family Services Family First Initiative: Progress report.* Chicago: Author

Feldman, L. (1990). *Evaluating the impact of family preservation services in New Jersey.* Trenton: Bureau of Research, Evaluation and Quality Assurance, New Jersey Division of Youth and Family Services.

Illinois Department of Children and Family Services. (1988). *Request for proposals to provide family preservation services.* Springfield: Author.

Kinney, J., Haapala, D. A., Booth, C., & Leavitt, S. (1991). The homebuilders model. In E. M. Tracy, D. A. Haapala, J. Kinney, & P. J. Pecora (Eds.), *Intensive family preservation services: An instructional sourcebook.* Cleveland, OH: Case Western Reserve University, Mandel School of Applied Social Sciences.

Littell, J. H., Schuerman, J. R., & Rzepnicki, T. L. (1991, April). *Preliminary results from the Illinois Family First Experiment: A quarterly report on the evaluation of the Family First Placement Prevention Project submitted to the Illinois Department of Children and Family Services.* Chicago: Chapin Hall Center for Children.

Maluccio, A. N., & Fein, E. (1985). Permanency planning revisited. In M. J. Cox & R. D. Cox (Eds.), *Foster care: Current issues, policies and practices* (pp. 113-133). Norwood, NJ: Ablex.

Marshall, T. H. (1964). *Class, citizenship, and social development.* Chicago: University of Chicago Press.

McDonald, W. R., & Associates. (1990). *Evaluation of AB 1562 in-home care demonstration projects (Vols. 1-3).* Sacramento, CA: Author.

Nelson, K. (1990, Fall). How do we know that family based services are effective? *The Prevention Report,* pp. 1-3.

Rzepnicki, T. L. (1991). Enhancing the durability of intervention gains: A challenge for the 1990s. *Social Service Review, 65*(1), 92-111.

Rzepnicki, T. L., Schuerman, J. R., & Littell, J. H. (1991). Issues in evaluating intensive family preservation services. In E. M. Tracy, D. A. Haapala, J. Kinney, & P. J. Pecora (Eds.),

Intensive family preservation services: An instructional sourcebook. Cleveland, OH: Case Western Reserve University, Mandel School of Applied Social Sciences.

Schuerman, J. R., Rzepnicki, T. L., & Littell, J. H. (1990, November). *Evaluation of the Illinois Department of Children and Family Services Family First Initiative: Progress report.* Chicago: Chapin Hall Center for Children.

Schuerman, J. R., Rzepnicki, T. L., & Littell, J. H. (1991). From Chicago to Little Egypt: Lessons from an evaluation of a family preservation program. In K. Wells & D. E. Biegel (Eds.), *Family preservation services: Research and evaluation.* Newbury Park, CA: Sage.

Weissert, W. G. (1988). The national channeling demonstration: What we knew, know now, and still need to know. *Health Services Research, 23*(1), 175-187.

Weissert, W. G., Cready, C. M., & Pawelak, J. E. (1988). The past and future of home- and community-based long-term care. *The Milbank Quarterly, 66*(2), 309-369.

Yuan, Y.-Y. T., & Rivest, M. (1990). *Preserving families: Evaluation resources for practitioners and policymakers.* Newbury Park, CA: Sage.

PART III

Special Populations

8

Supporting HIV Infected Children in Their Own Families Through Family-Centered Practice

JEAN ADNOPOZ
STEVEN F. NAGLER

Background

The need of all children for a consistent, nurturing relationship with a primary adult caregiver has long been recognized (Freud, 1965; Solnit, 1968). However, parental stressors such as disease, poverty, isolation, chemical dependency, and constitutional inadequacies and impairments can seriously affect the adults' capacity to parent successfully enough to avoid poor developmental, psychological, and educational outcomes for their children (Adnopoz, Nagler, & Grigsby, 1991). Daro (1990) and others have suggested that home visitor programs are among the most common strategies currently being employed to alter inappropriate behavior of parents under stress.

In 1985 the Yale Child Study Center created the Family Support Service in collaboration with the Connecticut Department of Children and Youth Services (DCYS). The program was established as an experimental time-limited and home-based model of family preservation service for families in which a child was identified by DCYS as being at imminent risk of out-of-home placement. The goals of the Family Support Service are to assess the family's ability to care for the child at risk, prevent placement when possible, and identify the community resources that can be utilized by the family upon discharge to maintain an improved level of functioning.

Using a mental health framework to inform child welfare service, the program pairs master's level clinicians with family support workers to assess the underlying individual and family dynamics, identify existing strengths and vulnerabilities; formulate a plan of intervention; and access concrete services.

The program was funded initially by the Edna McConnell Clark Foundation, which at that time had intensified its efforts to interest states in developing family preservation programs as a means of keeping children at high risk of out-of-home placement from entering the foster care system. As of 1987, the program has been funded by a yearly contract with the Department of Children and Youth Services.

In 1988 the incidence of pediatric HIV infection in New Haven, Connecticut, was 48.9 per 100,000, dramatically higher than in other communities of similar size. The provision of optimal medical care for these children was complicated by the adverse psychological and social factors that characterized their families and further affected their functioning.

As these first HIV infected children began to appear in the Family Support Service (FSS), it became apparent that although there were many similarities among the risks faced by noninfected and infected children and families, there were some crucial differences. Significant among these differences were the chronic nature of the psychosocial stress that HIV infection causes and the social stigma of the infection itself. In addition, medical issues were always involved in these cases and were often in the forefront.

Primarily, as a result of these factors, many HIV infected children were not receiving regular, prescribed health care. Care would frequently be episodic and crisis oriented. Children required stabilization in a hospital for problems that might have been prevented if rates of compliance with outpatient care had been higher. Not only did these inpatient stays demand the unnecessary separation of the child from his or her parent(s), they were costly and were not always medically necessary.

One of the first set of responses by the child welfare community to caring for children with HIV infection was to attempt to place children outside of the biological family—usually within the foster care system. When foster homes willing to undertake the care of fatally ill children were not available, a phenomenon known as "boarder babies." Children remained in hospitals for months at a time even though hospitalization was not medically necessary. As a result, children who were already vulnerable and subject to the trauma of life-threatening illness were being separated from their mothers and the historical and psychological continuity they represented. They were additionally burdened by a foster care system that could not respond to their numbers or needs.

The Family Support Service believed that such separations can be avoided if support is available and outpatient care stabilized. Children suffering from HIV infection have the same need for parental constancy, for love, and for nurture as all other children. Although their parents are also suffering from disease as well as other social and psychological stresses, they can be helped to care for their children, meet their needs, and function adequately in a parental role.

To enable these parents to care sufficiently for their children, access appropriate health care for all members of the family who need it, and avoid unnecessary separations, the family support service model was adapted to meet the specific needs of families and children infected with HIV virus.

Population

Pediatric AIDS is experienced chiefly by families who are already struggling with issues of poverty, drug use, and social isolation. The mothers of these children are often unmarried, young, poor women of color who are infected with the disease themselves. They may be physically ill. They are often clinically depressed and/or chronically psychologically depleted. Continuing drug use may place them and their children at further risk. Most significantly, denial and/or guilt about the infection often leads to a reluctance to follow through on medical care for themselves and for their children.

Infected mothers must struggle with their psychological reactions to their transmission of the disease to some of their children, their abandonment—through death—of all their children, as well as their own fears of death and dying. Once affected by HIV, the entire family is vulnerable to the negative social, psychological, and developmental effects of the disease.

Not surprisingly, individuals within such families attempt to cope with these major stressors in numerous ways. Unfortunately, when these strategies fail, individual family members may experience loss of self-esteem, depression, and anxiety accompanied by withdrawal and social isolation, and may tend to distrust those whom they feel do not understand them or meet their needs. For example, a common phenomenon observed in families with whom we currently work is their need to keep the diagnosis of AIDS a secret, not only from external, nonrelated persons, but also from family members, including infected and non-infected children as well as other adult members of the family.

In addition, the natural history of HIV infection in children has not yet been fully described. Short-term prognosis is difficult to determine and the course of the illness in children, as in adults, is uneven and unpredictable. As new treatments become available in the care of HIV exposed children and parents, they create the need for constant adaptations and adjustments. Although designed for the infected adult or child, these interventions affect everyone in the family. It is under these difficult conditions that HIV infected women, HIV exposed children, and even their uninfected siblings struggle to maintain a sense of emotional equilibrium and to lead their everyday lives. The effects of this struggle often contribute to increased depression and withdrawal, and increased, even frenzied, drug use.

The social stigma of the disease isolates families from their existing social networks. The effect of these additional stresses on many already fragile families can be overwhelming.

Thus basic needs of infected children for medical care, nutrition, hygiene, nurture, and developmental stimulation cannot be addressed without acknowledging the social and psychological needs of their families.

Program Adaptation

It was against this backdrop that the Family Support Service for HIV infected children and their families was begun in July of 1989 with an initial grant from the Public Welfare Foundation. In response to the episodic nature of the progression of HIV infection, the short-term, highly focused, intensive family preservation model of the Family Support Services was expanded both by the addition of a nurse and by a redefinition of the time frame for delivery of services.

The HIV program employs a team composed of a family support worker, a clinical social worker, and a nurse from the Visiting Nurse's

Association. The program attempts simultaneously to address both the child's and parent's concrete and clinical needs.

The relationship between the parent and family support team is the vehicle for clinical understanding, concrete support, and behavior change. Through an active focus on forming, expanding, and enhancing the relationship with the adult who is caring for the child (most often the mother or the grandmother), services are delivered along multiple axes at flexible levels of intensity.

At the heart of this relationship-based approach are the family support workers, whose backgrounds and communities are similar to those of the families served by the program. Family Support Workers bring to the work the experience of successful parenting in difficult circumstances; experience in negotiating informal and formal social systems; credibility through that experience; connections in the community; and a strong sense of affiliation with their clients. They are recruited, trained, and closely supervised within the program. It is largely through their ability to form and sustain relationships with parents who are fearful, isolated, and alienated that the program is able to provide or broker the necessary social, psychological, and medical services that enable children to remain at home despite their illness and other critical stressors.

The clinician on the team often is able to become involved with the parent only after a relationship with the family support worker and the parent has begun. The clinician then must establish a separate and distinct, but complementary role. Due to a sense that the clinician is both trustworthy and an "outsider" who has been initially vouched for by the more familiar family support worker, the parent is often able to discuss more easily her fears, fantasies, and deeper concerns.

It is common for the clinician to help the client to understand the medical aspects of HIV virus infection, and what it means to her to learn that she is infected and that she has infected her child. The complexity of the emotional conflicts for mothers who give birth to an HIV+ infant is most commonly seen in the mothers' differential responses to health care needs. With the team's support, mothers can frequently be motivated to obtain necessary medical care for the child. However, it is far less likely for mothers to achieve the same level of motivation to seek medical attention for themselves.

Thus an important and essential role of the clinician is to help the mother overcome her resistance to obtaining help for herself, whether it be to enter drug treatment, or to access regular medical care, or other appropriate resources. To achieve these ends the clinician might employ a range of strategies, including establishing regular individual contact, assessing the developmental needs of the children, arranging appropriate community referrals, and conducting beginning individual and family therapy in the home.

The visiting nurse plays a critical role on the team as the link between the hospital-based AIDS Care Clinic and the home. The nurse is able to interpret the multiple medical and physical parameters of HIV infected children's care for the family and the team. She is able to assist the parent with medication administration, nutritional management, and infection control procedures, at the same time that she is able to monitor the child's physical status. The presence of the nurse on the team enables the program to address more effectively the full range of psychological, psychosocial, and medical needs of HIV infected children and their parents.

Expanding the Definition of Family

In addition to the more traditional services, both concrete and clinical, a further elaboration of the family preservation model stimulated by this population is an initiative to expand the definition of *family* in order to create a system of care that can respond to a child's need for affection, stimulation, nurturing, and consistency of caregivers in more than one household at the same time. With mothers who are infected and often ill, grandmothers who are elderly and in uncertain health, and/or mothers who may be periodically impaired by their drug use, HIV+ children are at high risk for multiple, temporary, out-of-home placements.

In an attempt to minimize a child's experience of sudden disruption and abandonment, and to help parents address the issues of the child's future care and custody, the program has developed a practice of helping families identify an additional "expanded" family for its children when necessary. This family may be that of a relative, a neighbor, or a friend with whom the children can develop a meaningful bond, or a foster home that could commit to a relationship with a child that could endure beyond the death of the parent. In some cases this expanded family may function as the primary residence for the child(ren) while the(ir) mother visits or cares for the(ir) child(ren) when she is able. In others, the expanded family may operate as a respite care home used during periods of acute illness or fatigue. In all instances, the work of the program focuses on helping the adults to share, understand, and meet the needs of the child(ren). This often involves working through the dynamics of jealousy, guilt, and possessiveness between the two households. It also may mean addressing the practical aspects of sharing entitlement payments.

Some children may live with relatives in other geographic locations while maintaining periodic contact with mothers no longer able to care for them on a daily basis.

For many parents, planning for their child's future means that they must acknowledge the reality of their own imminent death. It forces into view feelings of guilt, shame, anger, and despair. The team of clinician, family support worker, and nurse, along with other caregivers, provide supportive and reality-based relationships in which these issues can be confronted without overwhelming parents and increasing their level of denial.

In all cases legal consultation and help with the preparation of wills is necessary for parents to achieve some control over future custody decisions. This can be accomplished through the pro bono efforts of private lawyers and a group of university law students.

Program Evaluation

The Family Support Service for HIV Infected Children illustrates the adaptive capacity of a short-term, highly focused, intensive family preservation program to expand its staff, its time frame, and its ability to support alternate care within a family paradigm. Initial evaluations of this model report a positive effect along the three major program parameters.

To assess the effects of the program on compliance with medical care, the outpatient clinic appointments from the Pediatric AIDS Program of Yale-New Haven Hospital from July 1989 to March 1990 and from April 1990 to January 1991 were reviewed. The proportion of times for which a child showed up for appointments after enrollment in the program was compared to the 1-year period prior to enrollment or, in instances where the child was younger than 1 year, the period of time since birth.

Prior to enrollment in the program, only 55% of the outpatient clinic appointments had been kept. Following enrollment in the program, the first period's compliance rate increased to 70%. In examining this data further, it was discovered that four families accounted for a large proportion of the missed appointments—they had only kept 41% of the appointments given. The other families had kept 88% of their appointments since enrollment. This review was then repeated for the period April 1, 1990 to January 15, 1991. The overall rate of kept appointments was positive—75%. Again, when the four families with the poorest rates were separated out, the rate of kept appointments of the remaining families reached 85%.

Another measure of the effectiveness of the program is the number of times that children have needed to be hospitalized. If the caregiver for a child is better able to provide for the child's general needs and sees to it that the child receives appropriate medical care and administers medications as prescribed, we would expect that the child's health would be improved and he or she would be hospitalized less frequently. In the first year and a half of operation there were only nine HIV-related hospitalizations among the 33 children sampled.

A third measure of effectiveness is whether or not children are able to continue to live with their families. Since the program began, there have been only two out-of-home foster care placements of children in the program.

Funding

Financial support of the Pediatric AIDS program was initially provided by the Public Welfare Foundation, which like the Edna McConnell Clark Foundation—the original funding source of the Family Support Service—acted as an agent for service change. The interest of both Foundations in creating new models of care for children at high risk provided support for the developers of the program and enabled them to focus on the work during the critical early stages of program development. Second-stage funding for the Pediatric AIDS program has come from the Connecticut Primary Care Association, which has accessed funding from the Federal Bureau of Maternal and Child Health to maintain the original program and to increase the referral and service network to include two community health clinics in New Haven and two additional sites in Bridgeport.

Ongoing funding is being sought actively from the Connecticut Department of Health both to maintain the current level of service and to support expansion as the AIDS epidemic extends. In addition to the significant psychosocial benefits, cost savings implications resulting from reduced hospitalizations and out-of-home placements, and increased compliance with medical regimen and appointments argue in favor of public support for preserving and strengthening HIV infected families.

Summary

Family preservation programs have demonstrated that they are able to reduce the rates of placement of children at high risk of removal from their biological homes because of abuse, neglect, or abandonment (Nelson, 1990; Nelson, Landesman, & Deutelbaum, 1990). An adaptation of one family preservation model, the Family Support Service, suggests that special needs populations, such as children and their parents infected with the HIV virus or with AIDS, can benefit physically and psychologically from intensive in-home relationship-based interventions designed to prevent out-of-home placement. By augmenting the clinician and family support worker team to include members of the AIDS Clinic medical staff and the local Visiting Nurse Association, a coordinated care package was developed for each child and parent referred to the program. The flexibility of the team model renders it particularly well suited to adaptations that reflect the specialized needs of specific target populations. However, certain underlying assumptions remain consistent across all family support models. These include an understanding of the child's need for the constancy of a primary caregiving relationship, for safety, and for protection; and the parents' need for support and validation as parents. The family support model offers promise as an effective intervention with families who find themselves faced with the possibility of disintegration as a result of medical, economic, psychosocial, or educational distress. Maintaining the integrity of the family throughout the intervention prevents undue trauma to already stigmatized and vulnerable children. The presence of the family support team within the home alleviates concerns about the child's safety, which are necessarily present in all cases where placement issues are raised, and allows for a comprehensive assessment of the needs of both child and family.

However, despite well-reasoned theory and promising program results, the notion of risk belies certainty. Clinicians and family support workers must grapple with the risk that their judgments and support may be inadequate or misinformed. They must rely on training, intuition, presumptions, and principles about what is in children's best interest to guide this and any family preservation practice. After all of that, the risks inherent in the work must be accepted.

References

Adnopoz, D. J., Nagler, S. F., & Grigsby, R. K. (1991). Multiproblem families and high-risk children and adolescents. In M. Lewis (Ed.), *Child and adolescent psychiatry: A comprehensive textbook* (pp. 1059-1066). Baltimore, MD: Williams & Wilkins.

Daro, D. (1990). Prevention of child physical abuse. In R. Ammerman & M. Hersen (Eds.), *Treatment of family violence* (pp. 331-353). New York: John Wiley.

Freud, A. (1965). Safeguarding the emotional health of the child. In J. Goldstein & J. Katz (Eds.), *The family and the law.* New York: Free Press.

Nelson, K. E. (1990, Fall). How do we know that family based services are effective? *The Prevention Report,* pp. 1-3.

Nelson, K. E., Landesman, M. T., & Deutelbaum, W. (1990). Three models of family-centered placement prevention services. *Child Welfare, 69,* 3-21.

Solnit, A. (1968). In the best interest of the child and his parents. In M. Levitt & B. Rubenstein (Eds.), *Orthopsychiatry and the law: A symposium* (pp. 139-155). Detroit: Wayne State University Press.

PART IV

Evaluation

9

Promoting Evaluation Research in the Field of Family Preservation

BRUCE A. THYER

Within the field of family preservation, as in many other areas within the human services, practice has by far outstripped research. The ever increasing demand to *do something* to alleviate the problems associated with familial breakup has engendered the rapid development and adoption of large-scale service programs devoted to maintaining families, programs costing millions of dollars in some cases, within individual states (see Wald, 1988). A number of proprietary concerns now market various intervention packages aimed at the "family preservation market," and franchise-like arrangements can be made with these firms to provide training in various models of family preservation. Alternatively, some states or localities "go it alone" and develop their own "in-house" family preservation service programs, utilizing local talent and knowledge to serve families in need.

Whether disseminated by existing programs or developed locally, most often such family preservation programs are based upon some theory or combination of conceptual frameworks that are seen as appropriate by the administrators in charge of developing and/or adopting such programs. For example, the Families First program is based on crisis intervention theory (cf. Barth, 1990, Holliday & Cronin, 1990; see also Golan, 1978). As Grigsby points out in Chapter 2 of this book, other theories that have gone into the development of intensive family preservation services (IFPS) include family systems theory, social learning theory, ecological theory, and functional theory, among others.

If the past is any guide, it seems likely that most if not all of these theories will eventually be shown to involve incorrect assumptions about family processes. Because the theories that most IFPSs are based upon guide the conceptualization of family functioning, the assessment process, and the provision of social service interventions, our views of family functioning, approaches to assessment, and the design of services are likely to prove faulty, ineffective at best, and perhaps harmful to our clientele. Moreover, the selection of programs (and their accompanying theoretical foundations) by states or human service agencies is not likely to have been guided by an exhaustive review of the available alternative IFPS programs. Rather, a selling job is often made by someone—perhaps a state employee, an agency staff member, or an outside "consultant," touting the virtues of a particular approach—who is successful in convincing the powers that be to adopt program "X" as the official IFPS program for a given agency, city, or state. The politics involved in the selection and adoption of various human service programs are well known to those familiar with the administrative decision-making process, and IFPSs are not exempt from such factors.

A number of outcome studies in the field of family preservation have been published in archival sources such as books and professional journals (e.g., Berry, 1992; Fraser, Pecora, & Haapala, 1991; Nelson, 1991; Wells & Biegel, 1991; Yuan & Struckman-Johnson, 1991), but the majority of such studies seem to take the form of internal reports and state-sponsored monographs, dissemination sources of much less value to the field due to their relative lack of accessibility and of careful external peer review prior to publication (e.g., Chapin Hall Center, 1991; Feldman, 1990; Florida Department of Health, 1990; Landsman, 1985; Mitchell, Tovar, & Knitzer, 1989; Remy & Hanson, 1982; Schuerman, Rzepnicki, & Littell, 1990; Showell, Hartley, & Allen, 1987). This is not to deny the value of such reports as possibly containing valid and useful findings, but their value as scientific documents is considerably less, relative to peer-reviewed archival publication outlets.

It is clear that given the social significance of the problems that IFPSs seek to address, the vast resources going into the provision of such services, and the concurrent lack of well-crafted evaluative research that demonstrates that these programs are truly effective (see Cole & Duva, 1990, pp. 79-95; Magura, 1981; Nelson, 1990; Yuan, McDonald, Wheeler, Stuckman-Johnson, & Rivest, 1990), a strong case can be made for human professionals active in the IFPS field to undertake systematic efforts toward the evaluation of their own programs.

How Does Evaluation Research Differ From Social Science Research?

The field of evaluation research is rapidly becoming known as a specialized form of scientific inquiry that presents the human service professional with unique challenges above and beyond those associated with other research endeavors. A distinction can be made between evaluation research and social science research in that the former has a more limited goal than the latter. In evaluation research we are interested in answering some relatively simple questions: "Did my client (family, group, agency, etc.) improve during or after receiving services?"—or, more ambitiously—"If my client did improve, was it the services my agency provided that are responsible for these positive changes?" Any conclusions to be drawn likely pertain *only* to the individuals or families under study (such as the participants in a local IFPS program). On the other hand, social science research typically is aimed at developing generalizable knowledge, or findings about psychosocial phenomena that are generally valid.

Note that most human service agencies and the providers of such services are more keenly interested in the former types of questions rather than in the latter, hence the contention made by this author (Harrison & Thyer, 1988; Thyer, 1989) and others that for the practicing human service professional, models of social science research are not as useful or relevant as those pertaining to evaluation research. Joel Fisher nicely defines *evaluation research* as studies that focus on "finding, developing and evaluating the methods of intervention that best help us do our job" (1980/1981, pp. 77-78). For example, a study of the psychosocial characteristics of physically abusive parents, or of the differences between abused and nonabused children, may be fine pieces of social science research, but they are not about helping people, which is the focus of evaluation research. On the other hand, examining the proportion of families who remain intact after receiving IFPS could be construed as an applied or evaluative study, one that may afford direct and practical guidance toward helping families. Because of our prior research training, tradition, and the comparative ease of conducting survey studies, too many researchers in the human services undertake social science-type projects in lieu of outcome studies. Given the importance of outcome studies to the field of family preservation work, the balance of this chapter will present some guidelines on the conduct of preliminary evaluation studies for workers in the field of IFPS to use in the design and conduct of such studies.

Practical Suggestions to Promote Evaluation Research in the Field of Family Preservation

Avoid Complex Research Designs

The design and conduct of evaluation research within the field of family preservation can be viewed as a progressively more complex series of questions to be answered, questions depicted in Table 9.1. The first such question seems relatively innocuous: "Did families improve over the course of (or after) intensive family preservation services?" My impression is that family preservation workers contemplating the conduct of evaluation research often overlook initially answering the evaluation question and instead tend to try to design studies appropriate to answering the experimental, comparative effectiveness, or componertial analysis questions. This is a serious mistake because the development of a research study capable of answering these latter questions is considerably more complex, involved, and difficult than one aimed at finding an answer to the evaluative question.

I believe that most human service workers (and agency programs) have not adequately answered the evaluative question. In other words, those of us involved in the provision of direct services do not have sufficient evidence that our families/clients are improved following treatment, yet this is the most fundamental issue involved in practice research. The difficulties involved in any premature attempt to conduct experimental, comparative effectiveness, or componential analytic studies may serve to convince budding practitioner researchers that the entire endeavor is too difficult or poses unsurmountable obstacles, and to abandon *any* further effort toward conducting evaluative research on family preservation programs.

To illustrate, to answer the question "What proportion of families receiving the 'Home First' program (a hypothetical example of an IFPS) are intact 6 months after services are terminated?" can be accomplished with a single-group posttest-only group research design, using a conve-

Table 9.1 Hierarchy of Research Questions and Relevant Designs for Use in Evaluating Family Preservation Programs.

1. What proportion of families receiving our IFPS remain intact? [This could be called the "evaluation" question]

Relevant Designs

Group	Single-System
X-O or O-X-O	"B" or "A-B"

2. Do our families (clients) improve *because of* our IFPS? [This could be called the "experimental" question]

Relevant Designs

Group	Single System
"O-X-O"	"A-B-A" or "A-B-A-B" or
O O	"multiple baseline designs"

3. Is family preservation program X better than family preservation program Y? [This could be called the "comparative effectiveness" question]

Relevant Designs

Group	Single-System
"O-X-O"	"A-B-A-C" or
O-Y-O	"Alternating Treatments Design"
O O	

4. What are the critical ingredients to the success of our family preservation program? [This could be called the "componential analysis" question]

Relevant Designs

Group	Single-System
"O-X (total) – O"	"A-(BC)-A-B-A-C-A"
O-X (-1) – O	etc.
etc.	

nience sample of clients receiving services at a given agency. For added elegance, pretest measures could be added, to result in a single-group pretest-posttest design. In the posttest-only study, simple descriptive statistics could be employed to analyze the data (i.e., "Six months after terminating from the Home First program, 87% of the families had remained intact"). This relatively simple information would be *very valuable* to know, particularly if you are a program administrator trying to obtain an increase in funding! If the pretest-posttest design were used, simple inferential statistics (e.g., a *t* test) could be employed to examine potential changes in the indirect outcome measures, such as social support and parenting skills scales (see Pecora, Fraser & Haapala, 1990, for an example of such a study). If a practitioner was intensively working with a single family, a "B" single-system design could be used, with the family members completing a family environment scale on a weekly basis, and the data graphically displayed to reveal (hopefully) improvements occurring over time. No inferential statistics would be needed at all to answer the question, "Has family adaptability and cohesion improved in the Stuart family while they have been participating in the Home First program?" Again, such information has obvious relevance clinically, and in the aggregate, programmatically.

To attempt to answer the second-level, or experimental question, one needs complex designs that intrude considerably more into service delivery functions. For example, to answer the question "Are the improvements seen in families receiving the Home First program brought about *only* by the program, and for no other plausible reason?" one would need a pretest-posttest no-treatment control group design, with half the families randomly assigned *not* to receive services, while the other half received the Home First program (see Table 9.1, point 2). Such a study could control for the possibility that the mere passage of time was responsible and thus provide stronger evidence that it was the formal program that produced the observed improvements. However, to do such a study you would need *twice* the number of families, families willing to be randomly assigned *not* to receive family preservation services. To design a study that would control for the effects of testing (another potential threat to internal validity) a Solomon four-group design would be needed, using four times as many families, randomly assigned to four differing conditions of treatment, no-treatment, and/or assessment.

To conduct a study capable of answering the third-level question, that of comparative effectiveness—such as "Is the Home First program more effective than the Family Builders program?"—you might need three times as many families, randomly assigned to receive Home First, or Family Builders, or no treatment at all. To answer the fourth-level question, that of componential analysis, such as "What are the critical ingredients to the Home First program?", a placebo control-group design could first be conducted, then a series of separate studies that compare the *entire* Home First program, consisting of say, intensive case management, the provision of concrete services, parent training, individual counseling, and family therapy, with another group of families receiving all of the Home First program *except* one element (say family therapy). If the families receiving the partial program improved as much as those receiving the entire program, then it could be concluded that the missing element is not a critical one to the success of the Home First program, and could perhaps be eliminated (to save resources).

Obviously the requirements and difficulties associated with answering Questions 2, 3, and 4 are exponentially larger than those involved in answering Question 1. In keeping with the philosophy embodied in such politically correct phrases as "Small is beautiful" and "Think globally, act locally," I suggest that family preservation workers contemplating the design and conduct of research on practice initially undertake relatively simple studies with the limited objective of determining whether or not their families are better off following IFPS than they were before. In conventional group research designs this could involve using posttreatment only single-group designs (X-O), or pretest-posttest single-group designs (O-X-O). In the field of single-system research designs the "B" and "A-B" designs are usually sufficient to answer the evaluative question, "Did my family improve following intensive family preservation services?" These recommendations appear to be consistent with the actual practices of clinicians who do make use of single-system research designs, according to a recent survey study by LeCroy and Tolman (1991).

I feel that such local-level evaluations are necessary even when a practitioner or agency adopts a method with considerable prior outcome studies supporting its efficacy. Even if prior research has shown the Home First model to be an effective family preservation program, it is still important that the practitioners and agency administrators providing such a program locally routinely conduct small-scale single-system or group outcome studies.

Sometimes it is indeed possible to conduct experimental, comparative effectiveness or componential analysis studies. For example, Lee and Holland (1991) used a no-treatment control group design to evaluate the effectiveness of a structured and widely used parent training program, as did Barber (1992), but the clinical and logistical opportunities for such efforts are comparatively rare. My call for more simply designed studies within the field of family preservation, conducted by the practitioners and administrators providing such services, should not be interpreted as equivalent to an abandonment of complex investigations, but as a recognition that the field can benefit immensely from simple evaluative research, and that experimental studies are not necessarily always feasible.

Have Clearly Defined and Limited Goals

In the arcane language of the research methodologist, the outcome measures for a given family preservation program are called the "dependent variables." Having said that, forget it, and from now on let's make exclusive use of the user-friendly term *outcome measure*. Outcome measures in the field of family preservation can be roughly grouped into two categories: *direct* and *indirect* measures. Now clearly the focus of family preservation programs is on helping families remain intact, or to reunite them as rapidly as possible if separations are necessary. The determination of the status of families who have received IFPS some time after such services have been terminated can be viewed as the most direct and useful measure of the "success" of such programs. Virtually all program evaluations of IFPS should include family status as a major indicator of the success of a given program.

The quality of the family environment is also an important factor, however, and a variety of family assessment methods have been developed that can be employed to assess systematically this aspect of program outcome (Fraser [1990] provides a nice introductory review of such potential outcome measures). Examples of such measures include the Child Well-Being Scales, Family Risk Scales, the Family Adaptability and Cohesion Scales, the Child Behavior Checklist, the Family Environment Scales, and various measures of social support, parenting skills, measures of parental or child psychopathology, and so on. Other valuable resources that can provide guidance in selecting potential indirect outcome measures include Toulicatos, Perlmutter, and Strauss (1990), Corcoran and Fischer (1987), and Robinson, Shaver, and Wrightsman (1991).

The use of these various scales as outcome measures within the family preservation field is primarily a rational one, not an empirical one. As a not-so-hypothetical example (see Lovell & Hawkins, 1988), let us assume that prior research has shown that socially insular mothers are at a greater risk to abuse/neglect their children than noninsular parents. One aspect of a IFPS might be to promote the parents' development of more extensive social networks, and use as an outcome measure a scale assessing available social supports, a scale given to the parent before and after receiving IFPS. If the aggregated data across all service recipients indicated that social supports were appreciably increased following IFPS, it is tempting to conclude that the program is "success-ful," the reasoning being that if mothers prone to abuse are insular, then an intervention that reduces insularity will reduce the likelihood of abuse. Remember, however, that the major indicator of success in IFPS is avoidance of child placement outside the home; and improvements in parental social supports, while perhaps valuable in and of themselves, are at best an indirect measure of the potential of a given IFPS to prevent such placements. Any evaluation of a family preservation program that relies exclusively on indirect measures suffers from a lack of credibility because it has not clearly shown that child placements are prevented/reduced, the raison d'être of such programs.

Accordingly, it is a good practice to select at most three or four outcome measures (including the direct assessment of family intact-ness, posttreatment), rather than attempt to use 6, 10, or even more scales or other measures, particularly for the novice program evaluator. The researcher is likely to suffer from information overload, lose track of data, and fall under the spell of statistical mavens who persuade one to conduct multiple regression analyses to isolate so-called predictor variables! Keep in mind the level of question being asked—ideally something like "What proportion of families receiving the Home First program remain intact, 6 months after services are terminated?"—and do not be seduced into trying to answer more complex questions by well-intentioned consultants likely trained as social scientists, not as program evaluators.

Never Invent Your Own Outcome Measure

The novice program evaluator is often tempted to develop a new scale or survey instrument to assess the success of a IFPS. Avoid this temp-tation like the plague! The design and validation of a scale or survey is a major project in and of itself, and a program evaluation is NO PLACE to try to develop such a measure. If you ignore this advice and prepare your own scale, your entire study's results may be called into question because the reader will have no evidence that your new measure is a reliable or valid one. As a social work journal editor, I can attest to the fact that this is a major reason why manuscripts get rejected: a well-meaning practitioner constructs his or her own idiosyncratic scale, obtains interesting results, and tries to publish them. Invariably the reviewers note this fact, reject the study, and sadly suggest that next time the writer should use a previously published scale or outcome measure with well-established reliability and validity. Instead, select from among the plethora of available outcome measures (noted in the previous section) and use two or three of these.

Avoid Institutional Review Boards If Possible

A major impediment to the timely completion of evaluative research projects can be the effort required to prepare proposals and receive approval from university or hospital-based institutional review boards (IRBs), local committees charged with ensuring that participation in research by clients receiving family preservation services will not result in violations of confidentiality or expose families to any other type of risk (note: IRBs are usually established at institutions receiving federal funding. Private agencies do not usually possess such committees). I strongly suggest that the evaluation of regular family preservation services does *not* constitute research or experimentation on human beings as this is usually understood, but rather is an expected and essential component of regular practice in the human services. An exception to this principle would be where an agency or individual worker is developing a novel treatment approach whose efficacy has never been determined, and a formal research project is designed to test its efficacy. Such an intervention falls outside the pale of "common and accepted practice" and IRB review may be necessary.

I like the common example of the physician who regularly monitors a patient's responses to an antihypertensive drug, documents these in a chart, and graphically portrays the data and interprets them visually. Such data are often freely shared with one's professional colleagues and supervisors, and form an important element in the quality assurance programs of many hospitals, practitioner self-evaluations of intervention, and in educating patients and professionals alike. Similar evaluation activities may be taken in the medical and psychosocial treatment of diabetics (by monitoring blood sugar), substance abusers (by monitoring urine test results), and obese persons (recording weight, and in some programs, certain blood test results), all without recourse to IRB scrutiny. Without adopting other aspects of a medical model, I suggest that family preservation workers contemplating relatively simple evaluation studies adopt a similar perspective, regardless of whether the issue involves the prospective collection of data in a planned evaluation, or the retrospective collection of data from agency records. Clients are not put at risk through such evaluation efforts, and in no sense of the term are they being subjected to "experimentation." Accordingly, I suggest avoiding contact with IRBs entirely in such cases. My experience has been that if you ask IRB staff about a proposed project, their standard response is to request that you submit a written proposal for their review. This is often accompanied by bland assurances that this is purely for your own protection, that it is merely a rubber-stamp procedure, that you will receive an answer immediately, and so forth. Compliance with such suggestions violates one's professional autonomy; if you fall into the trap of subjecting your work to IRB review, such a process will inevitably require more time than projected as the committee meets to consider proposals in a leisurely manner that does not take into account student/university/clinical/agency/funding timetables.

Various other criteria, such as whether or not a study is intended for publication or if the practitioner plans to analyze the data using inferential statistics, have little bearing on the protection of human subjects and should not be determinants of whether a given project should be subject to IRB approval. Evaluation is a *component of practice,* subject to the same ethical standards regarding confidentiality as other aspects of the human services. We do not have IRBs review a practitioner's use of patient-related data in our teaching and supervision, the production in internal agency reports, or class papers. As professionals we assume that client rights to confidentiality will be respected. An increasing number of states extend to social workers, psychologists, and other human service workers the legal right of "privileged communication," implying that not only will the professionals respect the privacy rights of their clients, but also that the professionals cannot be compelled to disclose information obtained about families during the course of their practice. Ample precedent thus exists to support the contention that human service professionals can be expected to take into account client rights to privacy and protection in the course of their professional activities. I suggest that a similar view be extended to the conduct of practitioner-conducted evaluations of service. We may be wise to avoid entirely the term *research* when discussing projects of this type, and call such projects "evaluations of practice" or a "quality assurance study." The following statement summarizes my views in this matter:

> The collection of information about families and their functioning, including how they think, behave and feel, before, during and after receiving family preservation services, is an integral part of ethical and competent professional

practice. It is inappropriate to treat such endeavors as a form of "research" requiring external review and approval.

Avoid Theory

It is a virtual truism among research textbooks that *Theory* (spelled with a capital T and often mentioned in a reverent tone and accompanied by vague gestures of genuflection) guides the design and conduct of all studies and that an essential element of any research report is a discussion of the implications of the results in terms of one or more relevant theories. I always urge my students, consultees, and other colleagues to avoid construing a projected outcome study as a method to obtain support for a particular theory, even if the proposed intervention is clearly derived from one. My rationale for this heretical notion is pragmatic. A family preservation program may be quite effective even if the theory it is based upon is incompletely understood or even completely erroneous. A case in point may be the behavioral therapy called systematic desensitization, used in the treatment of certain anxiety disorders. The original theoretical mechanism for its success (documented in the late 1950s and early 1960s) was a physiological process called reciprocal inhibition. The efficacy of systematic desensitization was undoubted, but in the late 1960s additional studies clearly demonstrated that the mechanism of reciprocal inhibition was *not* the reason why systematic desensitization worked. All the positive outcome studies on systematic desensitization did not confirm reciprocal inhibition as the correct theory. Similarly, any positive outcome study for an IFPS based on a given theory does not provide compelling evidence of the validity of that theory. In general, studies independent of those involving the evaluation of outcome are necessary to corroborate the accuracy of a given theory. Given that in the fullness of time all of our existing theories of family preservation programs will likely have been shown to be wrong, a strong personal investment on the part of a program evaluator in conducting a study in order to show that a particular theory is correct is not a good practice, in my opinion.

Of course, our evaluation studies may not always provide proof of the efficacy of a given family preservation program. Such a negative result is subject to at least two interpretations. In the first, one may conclude that the theory the program is based upon is *wrong*. The logic is simple. If theory A predicts that treatment B will ameliorate problem C, treatment B is applied and C is unchanged, then theory A is incorrect.

However, the defenders of theory A will always claim that the service providers of treatment B were obviously incompetent, and *that* is the real reason why problem C was not helped. Therefore a negative outcome study rarely resolves the issue of the validity of a particular theory.

A further reason for my personal eschewal of theory in designing outcome studies is that in most cases I am consulting with students or agency staff on the evaluation of *existing* social service programs, not new innovative ones. These existing programs may be only tenuously tied to theory, and instead based more on state/agency policies, clinical wisdom and common sense, and tradition. Hence my students and I "begin where the client is at" in the sense that our "client" is the agency and we take the existing services they provide and work with the local practitioners in evaluating those services.

Actually, many services provided by human service professionals could be said to be theory-free: for example certain aspects of child protective services, case management, and the generalized and nonspecific counseling provided in our community mental health centers. When asked what theory they base their practice on, many practitioners respond with a vacuous look, rueful smile, or shrug. A number of empirical studies have documented the rather tenuous nature of this relationship between theory and practice. For example:

> Few of the social workers interviewed were able to give any indication that they were consciously applying any theoretical knowledge to their practice, and were rarely able to indicate in descriptions of their activities the concepts which guided them in carrying out their professional tasks. (Young, 1979, p. ix)

Kolevzon and Maykrantz (1982) and Sheldon (1978) have reached related conclusions. Nevertheless, it is a perfectly reasonable and practical undertaking to evaluate a family preservation program, regardless of its theoretical formulation, or even its absence.

This view of the irrelevance of theory is supported by a recent study that appeared in the *Journal of Consulting and Clinical Psychology,* which examined the theoretical foundations of psychotherapy outcome studies that had appeared in that top-ranked journal between 1967 and 1988. During the 1960s approximately 69% of such studies had a theoretical rationale, whereas in the 1970s and 1980s this percentage declined to about 30% (cf. Omer & Dar, 1992). Clearly the view that outcome studies and program evaluation research can be construed as a test of some psychosocial theory has become less commonplace in recent years.

Avoid Focusing on the Independent Variable

Our research texts usually provide advice to the effect that any well-designed study must specify the independent variable (i.e., treatment or interventive program) in a clear and replicable manner. I believe that this is unwise advice for the program evaluator to try to follow in conducting preliminary evaluations of a family preservation program. Usually both widely adopted and standardized as well as idiosyncratic agency-developed family preservation programs contain multiple elements, and always involve some aspects that are difficult to operationalize well. To pretend that we can capture all of the salient characteristics of a given type of program when conducting small-scale and uncontrolled evaluation studies is overly ambitious at best and deceptive at worst. Generally such efforts are reserved for the most rigorous type of practice-research, called "componential analysis" in Table 9.1, wherein one attempts to isolate the critical ingredients of a family-based intervention. This generally requires a degree of experimental control and resources beyond those of the autonomous practitioner or isolated agency, and such studies are best deferred, in my view. It is acceptable, and even valuable, in the early stages of research on practice to demonstrate that a given family preservation program is effective in helping clients, even if the exact particulars of that service are not clearly understood. It is only after the relevant evaluative studies have shown that *something* helpful is going on does it become worthwhile to go to the effort to specify the interventions adequately.

Avoid Qualitative Research Methods

Our literature has lately reflected an interest in the use of qualitative methodologies for use in evaluating programs. To date, however, the vast majority of such articles and chapters have limited themselves to describing the *potential* of such methods, and/or their purported advantages over quantitative methods. The numbers of published studies actually using qualitative methods, particularly within the field of research on family preservation programs, remains minuscule. Until I see more actual *demonstrations* of the use of qualitative methods as producing knowledge useful for this field I remain skeptical of their value and recommend that the budding program evaluator obtain a more thorough grounding in conventional quantitative methods, including group and single-system designs, and descriptive and inferential statistics (see Bickman, 1990).

In any event, my impression is that the major role of qualitative methods lies in their ability to help the practitioner-researcher generate testable *hypotheses* about family dynamics. Quantitative methods afford very little help in this regard—the *construction* of hypotheses. However, the *testing* of hypotheses is best achieved, in my view, through quantitative methods. I believe that the role of qualitative research methodologies will remain a minor and secondary one when it comes to evaluating the outcomes of family preservation programs for the foreseeable future.

Ignore Issues of External Validity

In conventional social science research we are taught the vital importance of obtaining a representative sample of subjects to do our study on, so that any findings may be logically and statistically generalized to the larger population from which the sample was drawn. Students, educators, and program evaluators often engage in considerable breast-beating over this issue, and may disparage a proposed or published evaluation of practice because of its use of a convenience sample rather than a randomly selected one. One often hears the use of single-system research designs criticized for this very reason, that any findings are of little importance since they cannot be generalized.

I feel that this is basically a nonissue. The fact is that NO ONE, to my knowledge, has ever employed a truly randomly selected sample of clients (or families) chosen from a larger population of interest, and conducted an outcome study using such clients. The actual practice is almost always to employ a convenience sample, selected on the basic of availability (such as clients seen at your agency). One may not generalize the findings from such studies to other clients with similar problems, *not matter how large the sample size.* A study done on 100 families selected on the basis of convenience in the town of Roosterpoop, Georgia, does not yield findings that can be extrapolated to all families, in Roosterpoop, in Georgia, or anywhere else.

In the field of research on practice one must usually be content to conduct a study that has *internal validity,* at best, and hope that external validity will eventually be demonstrated through independently conducted replication studies in the future. The moral here is that *all* evaluations of practice are likely to be seriously compromised in terms of external validity, and that this limitation similarly affects *both* group and single-system research designs. Be aware that the same problem exists for outcome studies conducted in fields such as psychology, psychiatry, and education. It is not something to be embarrassed about but recognized and eventually circumvented through replication research. This recommendation is further supported by a recent study by Downs and Robertson (1991) that raises significant questions about the generalizability of findings from random samples to clinical populations.

Summary

In this chapter I have tried to convey some practical suggestions for possible use by novice program evaluators in the field of intensive family preservation programs. A case was made for the importance of conducting evaluation research on these methods of assisting families, and for such studies to be undertaken by the service providers of these services themselves, as opposed to external consultants. The specific suggestions offered are expressed largely in the negative, being admonitions about practices to avoid. Avoid large and complex research designs; clearly delimit your goals; never invent and use your own outcome measures; avoid institutional review boards if at all possible; avoid designing studies with the intention of testing a theory; avoid an overemphasis on describing the interventive program in great detail; avoid attempting to employ qualitative research methods for the purposes of program evaluation; and ignore issues related to external validity (don't bother trying to generalize your findings).

In general I advocate the use of relatively simple group- and single-system research designs intended to answer the question, "Do families receiving this family preservation program benefit?" because obtaining data on this issue is of fundamental importance to service providers and administrators. Other more sophisticated research designs may be used to answer more complex evaluative questions, but it is usually premature to address these more complex issues until the simpler ones have been adequately answered. A major deterrent to the conduct of simple evaluative research studies by practitioners is the well-intended advice of colleagues trained in the conduct of social science research but ill-informed about the unique aspects of applied or evaluative studies, with such advice resulting in impractical designs beyond the capacity of agency-based practitioners to undertake, or the abandonment of evaluation efforts. Keep it simple, think small, be content with small wins, but just do it.

References

Barber, J. G. (1992). Evaluating parent education groups: Effects on sense of competence and social isolation. *Research on Social Work Practice, 2,* 28-38.

Barth, R. P. (1990). Theories guiding home-based intensive family preservation services. In J. K. Whittaker, J. Kinney, E. M. Tracy, & C. Booth (Eds.), *Reaching high risk families: Intensive family preservation in human services.* Hawthorne, NY: Aldine de Gruyter.

Berry, M. (1992). An evaluation of family preservation services: Fitting agency services to family needs. *Social Work, 37,* 314-321.

Bickman, L. (1990). Study design. In Y.-Y. T. Yuan & M. Rivest (Eds.), *Preserving families: Evaluation resources for practitioners and policymakers* (pp. 132-165). Newbury Park, CA: Sage.

Chapin Hall Center for Children. (1991, June). *Evaluation of the Illinois Department of Children and Family Services Family First Initiative: Progress report.* Chicago: Author.

Cole, E. & Duva, J. (1990). *Family preservation: An orientation for administrators and practitioners.* Washington, DC: Child Welfare League of America.

Corcoran, K. J., & Fischer, J. (1987). *Measures for clinical practice: A sourcebook.* New York: Free Press.

Downs, W. R., & Robertson, J. F. (1991). Random versus clinical samples: A question of inference. *Journal of Social Service Research, 14*(1/2), 57-83.

Feldman, L. (1990). *Evaluating the impact of family preservation services in New Jersey.* Trenton: Bureau of Research, Evaluation and Quality Assurance, New Jersey Division of Youth and Family Services.

Fischer, J. (1980/1981). Do research reviews contribute to knowledge development? The case of "Social service research: Reviews of studies." *Journal of Social Service Research, 4,* 77-78.

Florida Department of Health and Rehabilitative Services. (1990, December). Supplemental services: Intensive crisis counseling program (ICCP). In Florida Department of Health and Rehabilitative Services, *Outcome evaluation report.* Tallahassee: Author.

Fraser, M. (1990). Program outcome measures. In Y.-Y. T. Yuan & M. Rivest (Eds.), *Preserving families: Evaluation resources for practitioners and policymakers* (pp. 77-101). Newbury Park, CA: Sage.

Fraser, M. W., Pecora, P. J., & Haapala, D. A. (1991). *Families in crisis: The impact of intensive family preservation services.* Hawthorne, NY: Aldine de Gruyter.

Golan, N. (1978). *Treatment in crisis situations.* New York: Free Press.

Harrison, D. M., & Thyer, B. A. (1988). Doctoral research on social work practice. *Journal of Social Work Education, 24,* 107-114.

Holliday, M., & Cronin, R. (1990). Families first: A significant step toward family preservation. *Families in Society, 71,* 303-306.

Kolevzon, M. S., & Maykrantz, J. (1982). Theoretical orientation and clinical practice: Uniformity versus eclecticism. *Social Service Review, 56,* 121-129.

Landsman, M. J. (1985). *Evaluation of fourteen child placement prevention projects in Wisconsin, 1983-1985.* Iowa City: University of Iowa, National Resource Center on Family Based Services.

LeCroy, C. W., & Tolman, R. M. (1991). Single-system design use of behavior therapists: Implications for social work. *Journal of Social Service Research, 14*(1/2), 45-55.

Lee, J., & Holland, T. P. (1991). Evaluating the effectiveness of foster parent training. *Research on Social Work Practice, 1,* 162-174.

Lovell, M. L., & Hawkins, J. D. (1988). An evaluation of a group intervention to increase the personal social networks of abusive mothers. *Children and Youth Services Review, 10,* 175-188.

Magura, S. (1981). Are services to prevent foster care effective? *Children and Youth Services Review, 3,* 193-212.

Mitchell, C., Tovar, P., & Knitzer, J. (1989). *The Bronx homebuilders program: An evaluation of the first 45 families.* New York, NY: Bank Street College of Education.

Nelson, K. E. (1990, Fall). How do we know that family based services are effective? *The Prevention Report,* pp. 1 - 3.

Nelson, K. E. (1991). Populations and outcome in five family preservation programs. In K. Wells & D. E. Biegel (Eds.), *Family preservation services: Research and evaluation.* Newbury Park, CA: Sage.

Omer, H., & Dar, R. (1992). Changing trends in three decades of psychotherapy research: The flight from theory into pragmatics. *Journal of Consulting and Clinical Psychology, 60,* 88-93.

Pecora, P. J., Fraser, M. W., & Haapala, D. A. (1990, Fall). Intensive family preservation services: An update from the family based intensive treatment research project. *The Prevention Report,* pp. 4-5.

Remy, L. L., & Hanson, S. P. (1983). *Evaluation of the emergency family care program, San Francisco Home Health Service: Final report.* San Francisco: San Francisco Home Health Service.

Robinson, J. P., Shaver, P. R., & Wrightsman, L. S. (Eds.). (1991). *Measures of personality and social psychological attitudes.* New York: Academic Press.

Schuerman, J., Rzepnicki, T. L., & Littell, J. (1990, November). *Evaluation of the Illinois Department of Children and Family Services Family First Initiative: Progress report.* Chicago: Chapin Hall Center for Children.

Sheldon, B. (1978). Theory and practice in social work: A reexamination of a tenuous relationship. *British Journal of Social Work, 8,* 2-22.

Showell, W. H., Hartley, R., & Allen, M. (1987). *Outcomes of Oregon's family therapy programs: A descriptive study of 999 families.* Salem: State of Oregon Children's Services Division.

Thyer, B. A. (1989). First principles of practice research. *British Journal of Social Work, 19,* 309-323.

Toulicatos, J., Perlmutter, B. F., & Strauss, M. A. (Eds.) (1990). *Handbook of family measurement techniques.* Newbury Park, CA: Sage.

Wald, M. S. (1988, Summer). Family preservation: Are we moving too fast? *Public Welfare,* pp. 33-46.

Wells, K., & Biegel, D. E. (Eds.). (1991). *Family preservation services: Research and evaluation*. Newbury Park, CA: Sage.

Young, P. (1979). Foreword. In K. Curnock & P. Hardiker, *Towards practice theory*. London: Routledge & Kegan Paul.

Yuan, Y.-Y. T., McDonald, W. R., Wheeler, C. E., Struckman-Johnson, D., & Rivest, M. (1990). *Evaluation of AB 1562 in-home care demonstration projects: Final report*. Sacramento, CA: Walter R. McDonald & Associates.

Yuan, Y.-Y. T., & Struckman-Johnson, D. L. (1991). Placement outcomes for neglected children with prior placements in family preservation programs. In K. Wells & D. E. Biegel (Eds.), *Family preservation services: Research and evaluation*. Newbury Park, CA: Sage.

Epilogue

Family Preservation and Social Change

The Need for Future Dialogue

E. SUSAN MORTON
WILLIAM EYBERSE

This society is not taking care of its children and the result is that we are throwing away our future. We claim to be a child-centered nation but are guilty of unconscionable neglect and uncaring actions directed toward our children. The United States now leads all the major industrialized countries in the gap dividing the rich and the poor. The poorest group in our society is the children.

In one of the richest countries in the world, 20% of our children live in poverty. Malnutrition affects nearly half a million children. More than 12 million children have no health insurance. The United States ranks 19th in the world in preventing infant deaths, behind such nations as Spain, Ireland, Hong Kong, and Singapore. A growing number of children are homeless. It is estimated that as many as 100,000 children have no place to call home (Children's Defense Fund, 1990).

Classrooms are overcrowded and teachers are overburdened. The United States ranks 19th in the world for having the highest pupil to teacher ratio at 23 children to 1 teacher. Only one out of every six eligible children receives Headstart services. More than 500,000 children drop out of school each year. Seventy-five percent of those children are poor (Children's Defense Fund, 1990).

As poverty and stress increase so too does hopelessness, helplessness, family violence, family dissolution, substance abuse, teen pregnancy, and child abuse and neglect. Child abuse is only one part of a general phenomenon of mistreatment of children (Gil, 1973). For effective treatment and prevention to occur, it must be seen as a result of the interplay between individual behavior and the societal environment (social, economic, and political spheres) surrounding children and their families. Individual-level factors include the parents' personality; their own childhood experiences with exposure to abuse and neglect, lack of nurturing from others, and rejection by parents; and inappropriate developmental expectations for their children. Family factors involve the interactions between family members, the established roles of family members, and temperamental mismatch between the members. Stress caused by unemployment, lack of education, crime, lack of adequate housing and food, poor medical care, and isolation from social support systems are examples of community variables. Societal tolerance of violence and the legitimization of physical punishment to control children's behavior act at the cultural level to sanction abuse (Belsky, 1980).

Family preservation can be viewed as an ecological, competence-centered intervention that acknowledges the complexities of child abuse and poses factors and forces that create an abusive situation. It does this by concentrating on four realms: increasing knowledge, improving social competence, strengthening kinship/community relations, and advocacy. By focusing on these four areas preservation practitioners have had a direct impact on families. Their methods have resulted in the prevention of unnecessary placements, stabilization of crisis situations, maintenance and strengthening of family functioning and familial bonds, increase of the family's skills and competency, and facilitation of the family's use of formal and informal support resources.

Indirectly, the concentration on these four realms has produced results that impact our society on a larger scale. Innovative programs such as family preservation have provided us with invaluable information and increased our knowledge base regarding children and families. They have demonstrated that most families can function and that most at-risk children can remain at home if intensive services are provided. Programs such as these are charting the way for practice with children and families in the future.

Family preservation has also identified inefficiencies in the larger service delivery system and inconsistencies in the general public policy regarding children and families in this country. It has made us more aware that we are guilty of jeopardizing our children's futures and the future of this country by failing to address adequately the problems and issues relating to poverty, unemployment, sexism, racism, and ethnocentrism. Instead we continue to pursue shortsighted temporary policies that take away from our children's educational, emotional, and physical needs. We are at risk for producing a nation of social incompetents.

Through its concentration on community family preservation has strengthened our understanding of the need for social supports for families. The advocacy work has illustrated the complexity of the social, economic, and political systems in which families are embedded.

Family preservation's uniqueness is that it is a very specialized intervention that could be a vehicle for radical social reforms. In the future, family preservation's commitment to families must be broadened to include a commitment to social reform. Along with its ever evolving direct service work with children and their families, it must direct its attention toward changing this nation's priorities regarding children and their families. If it fails to do this, then it will be doing a grave disservice to the very clients that it seeks to serve.

References

Belsky, J. (1980). Child maltreatment: An ecological integration. *American Journal of Psychology, 35,* 320-335.

Children's Defense Fund. (1990). *Children 1990: A report card, briefing book, and action primer.* Washington, DC: Children's Defense Fund.

Gil, D. G. (1973). *Violence against children: Physical child abuse in the United States.* Cambridge, MA: Harvard University Press.

Index

About the Contributors

Kathleen Abate received an M.S.W. from Columbia University in 1986. She is currently a school social worker in the New Haven (CT) Public Schools. Previously she held an appointment as a Clinical Instructor in Social Work at the Yale Child Study Center, and served as a family preservation clinician in the Center's Intensive Family Preservation Service. She is a recipient of the Distinguished Service Award from the Connecticut Department of Human Resources, for her prior work with the elderly and people with disabilities, and recently completed a term on the Board of Directors of the Easter Seals Rehabilitation Center in New Haven.

Jean Adnopoz, M.P.H., is an Associate Clinical Professor and the Coordinator of Community Child Development and Child Welfare Programs at the Yale Child Study Center. She is a founder, with Steven F. Nagler, of the Family Support Service and the Family Support Service for HIV Infected Children at the Yale Child Study Center in New Haven, CT. She has been committed to the development of programs that have as their goal the maintenance of children at high risk of out-of-home placement within their biological families. Currently, the Family Support Programs that she coordinates are available to meet the needs of families in which children are reported as abused, neglected, or abandoned; families affected by HIV infection; and families in which parents are involved with substance abuse.

Marianne Berry, Ph.D., A.C.S.W., is an Assistant Professor at the University of Texas at Arlington School of Social Work, specializing in child welfare policy and programs. She is a Fellow of the American Association of University Women. She received a bachelor's degree in behavioral sciences and a master's degree in social service administration from the University of Chicago, and received her doctorate in social welfare from the University of California at Berkeley. She has published research on permanency planning outcomes, family preservation services, special needs adoption, and open adoption. She is the recipient of the Frank R. Breul Memorial Prize from the University of Chicago School of Social Service Administration for outstanding scholarship in child welfare.

Stephen Budde is Research Associate at the Chapin Hall Center for Children and a doctoral student at the School of Social Service Administration at the University of Chicago. He has worked in child welfare for 10 years as a therapist, administrator, researcher, and case manager. In addition to his work on the evaluation of family preservation programs, he is interested in the theory and development of risk assessment models in child welfare. His dissertation is a qualitative analysis of decisions regarding placement and referral to family preservation programs.

Sandra D. Erickson, B.S.W. graduate from the college of St. Scholastica in Duluth (MN), served as the permanency planning coordinator for the Minnesota Department of Human Services. She is currently the Deputy Chief of Dependency Programs for the State of Florida, with lead responsibility for statewide efforts to enhance the delivery of intensive family-based services.

William Eyberse, M.F.T., is the Coordinator of the Intensive Family Preservation Program at Child & Family Agency of Southeastern Connecticut in New London.

R. Kevin Grigsby, D.S.W., A.C.S.W., is an Assistant Professor of Social Work at the University of Georgia School of Social Work and an Assistant Clinical Professor in the Department of Psychiatry and Health Behavior at the Medical College of Georgia. He has worked in the field of family preservation since 1985. Over the past 6 years he has held positions as clinician, supervisor, trainer, and program coordinator in an intensive family preservation program. He has completed Homebuilders training, and has delivered family preservation services in both the single clinician model and the clinician-family support worker team model. His current research interests include family preservation, family reunification, and family support for grandparents who are the primary care providers for children.

Jeanne Howard is Associate Professor of Social Work at Illinois State University and a Research Associate with the family preservation evaluation at Chapin Hall Center for Children at the University of Chicago. She has written in the area of foster care and adoption and is currently evaluating the State of Illinois adoption preservation initiative. Her research interests include the treatment of siblings in foster care and empowerment issues in child welfare.

Julia H. Littell is Research Fellow at the Chapin Hall Center for Children at the University of Chicago and Project Director of the evaluation of family preservation programs in the State of Illinois. In addition, she had conducted research on the availability, use and long-term effects of extracurricular and community-based programs for children and youth. As the Director of Research for the Family Resource Coalition, she conducted national surveys of community-based family support and education programs and provided technical assistance on research and evaluation for service providers.

Kaarina Massarene, M.S.W., is a Clinical Instructor in Social Work at the Yale Child Study Center. She provides clinical social work services to children and their families through the Center's Intensive Family Preservation Service. She previously was the Program Director of the North Country Family Program of Northern New Hampshire Youth Services, in Littleton. She has extensive experience in providing home-based counseling, psychotherapy, and case management to varied populations in both inner-city and rural areas.

E. Susan Morton, A.C.S.W., is currently Clinical Director of Waterford Country School, a residential facility for emotionally and behaviorally disturbed children. She has worked in the area of family preservation since 1986, and has served as Director of Community Services at Child

& Family Agency of Southeastern Connecticut. She has worked in child welfare in both public and private settings doing prevention and treatment as a clinician, supervisor, educator, researcher, and administrator. Her current research interests include family preservation, family violence, substance abuse, and the relationships among them.

Steven F. Nagler, M.S.W., is an Assistant Clinical Professor of Social Work and Clinical Director of the Family Support Services at the Yale Child Study Center. He is a founder, with Jean Adnopoz, of the Family Support Service and the Family Support Service for HIV Infected Children at the Yale Child Study Center in New Haven, CT. He is also a consultant and trainer for the Connecticut State Department of Children and Youth Services and the New Haven Police Department. His work on the issues at the intersection of child mental health and child welfare have appeared in various journals and edited volumes.

Ann E. Quinn, M.S.W., is the acting Assistant Director of the Training Academy for the Connecticut Department of Children and Youth Services in Bridgeport, where she is responsible for the planning, scheduling, and coordinating of training offered to all DCYS staff. She has been with the Department since 1963 and until recently was in charge of Protective Service/Child Welfare operations in a regional office.

Tina L. Rzepnicki is Associate Professor at the School of Social Service Administration and Faculty Associate at the Chapin Hall Center for Children at the University of Chicago. She is Co-Principal Investigator of the Illinois family preservation and family reunification program evaluations. Her research and publications have addressed welfare decision making, empirically based practice with children and families, and maintenance of intervention effects. She co-authored *Decision Making in Child Welfare Services: Intake and Planning* (with Theodore J. Stein) and *Effective Social Work Practice* (with Elsie M. Pinkston and others).

Richard Schafer has a B.A. degree from Florida State University's School of Social Work, Tallahassee, and an M.A. degree in counseling from St. Thomas University, Miami. He is a program specialist for family preservation services for the State of Florida. He has assisted in the State's efforts to provide family preservation services statewide through the Intensive Crisis Counseling Program, was instrumental in the creation of the Intensive Family Services program, and helped in the formulation, legislation and creation of the Family Builders model. He is currently overseeing the comprehensive evaluation of the Family Builders first year of operation.

John R. Schuerman is Professor in the School of Social Service Administration at the University of Chicago, Faculty Associate at the Chapin Hall Center for Children, and editor of *Social Service Review*. He is Co-Principal Investigator of evaluations of the family preservation and family reunification programs of the State of Illinois. He is the author of *Research and Evaluation in the Human Services* and *Multivariate Analysis in the Human Services*. His other research interests include the investigation of the use of expert systems in social welfare decision making.

Charles R. Soulé is a lecturer at the Yale Child Study Center, and the Program Coordinator for the Center's Intensive Family Preservation Service. Previously, he was a Predoctoral Psychology Fellow in the Department of Psychiatry at Yale University School of Medicine. His clinical and research interests include services for high-risk children and families, the impact of social and parental expectations on children's social and academic development, and training and consultation to agencies serving at-risk children. He is completing a doctoral degree in Clinical and Community Psychology at the University of California at Berkeley.

Bruce A. Thyer is Professor of Social Work and Adjunct Professor, Department of Psychology, at the University of Georgia School of Social Work and Clinical Associate Professor of Psychiatry and Health Behavior, the Medical College of Georgia. He has published extensively in the area of behavioral social work and is the founding editor of the Sage journal, *Research on Social Work Practice*.